Imago Mundi

Imago Mundi

POEMS

Loren Wilkinson

Regent College Publishing
www.regentpublishing.com

Imago Mundi: Poems
Copyright © 2016 by Loren Wilkinson

Published 2016 by Regent College Publishing

Regent College Publishing
5800 University Boulevard
Vancouver, BC V6T 2E4
Canada

Regent College Publishing is an imprint of the Regent Bookstore
(www.regentbookstore.com).Views expressed in works published
by Regent College Publishing are those of the author and do
not necessarily represent the official position of Regent College
(www.regent-college.edu).

ISBN 978-1-57383-533-6

Cataloguing in Publication information is on file at Library and
Archives Canada.

"Christmas, Whidbey Island" has appeared in *HIS* / "Imago
Mundi" has appeared in the *Reformed Journal*

Front cover image of "That's How the Light Gets In" (pebbles
on wood, 12" x 16", 2001) by Brian Fee; photo by Alex Gust
/ Back cover image of Chapelle Saint-Gabriel by Mary Ruth
Wilkinson / Book design and layout by The Dunbar Group,
LLC (www.DunbarPublishing.com)

Contents

Foreword

Loren Wilkinson is one of those native souls to whom the tag "natural poet" adheres like pollen to a bee's knees. He has not made a career out of poetry—other things like teaching and farming have absorbed many of the years of his life—but his poems have accompanied him, tagging along like kids who look up to their dad and find his imaginative company a source of wisdom and wonder. His personal presence and his way of living are models of enthusiasm for the creation and its Creator.

Loren is a bit like Adam, discovering new beauty and interest in his environment, paying close and loving attention to the glints of splendor that swim into his vision every day. He names things in order to bring them to our attention.

Generous in his stewardship of people and property, yet humble and self-effacing, Loren has crafted skilful poetry out of the details that comprise the whole. I vividly remember a conversation that we had while we were grubbing up some encroaching Scotch broom from a path that overlooks the Trincomali Channel in the South Gulf Islands of British Columbia. Loren is good at this, inspiring people to want to work with him. Both of us were hot and sweaty but as we continued to bend and dig and grab more weeds Loren was vigorously commenting on an aspect of

Martin Heidegger's philosophy about which I'd been questioning him. His mind was as acutely at work as his body was busy.

One summer I was involved in a week of forging our way around the islands in a wooden ship's boat modeled after that of explorer Dionisio Galiano, for which the island on which the Wilkinsons make their home is named. This adventure, led by Loren and his valiant wife Mary Ruth, was embarked on during one of his Regent College summer school courses, "Wilderness, Creation and Technology." About 18 of us and our duffle bags were tightly packed into this craft along with our oars. We sang rowing songs as we learned to stroke in perfect precision. We traveled about 120 miles among the islands, braving rip tides and passing ferries. It rained every day. In spite of Goretex everything was damp except our spirits. Enthusiasm reigned.

Along the way Loren often consulted a tide table. Occasionally we felt that he deliberately had us rowing against the tide to develop our perseverance and rowing muscles. We'd feel triumphant when we could note a few yards of progress gauged by passing a moss-covered rock in a channel. We camped, soggily, on a different island almost every night. After the tents were set up and dinner had been prepared under a tarp and over a campfire, we would all sit around on rocks or stumps for the evening's discussion. Our task was to discuss impact of technology on our environment, that surrounded us, richly green and beautiful.

I have known Loren and Mary Ruth for many of the most meaningful years of my life. I've knitted sweaters for both of them. While visiting their home and farm on Galiano Island I've participated as they prepared sumptuous home-made soups and pastas with vegetables grown in their garden. I've watched them hosting individuals and large groups (their hospitality was legendary) for Island holiday weekends. I've been to church with them at St. Margaret's, the little Anglican church on Galiano. I have sat and talked poetry in his Regent classes on "The Christian Imagination." As mentor and friend to students Loren was a much-loved faculty member at the college for many fertile years. No one was better equipped than he to lead discussions of wide-ranging topics such as literature, poetry, theology, ecology and philosophy.

These imaginative strengths show up in this collection of poems, accumulated over the years, in which his Celtic sensibility shows up, joining spirituality and earthy sensuousness. In them he celebrates family, friends, our green planet and his great Friend, its Creator. One of my favourites, "The Necessity of Snowshoes" (p. 5) was for me a kind of beacon of personal experience translated into poetry. In that poem, a gesture to Robert Frost, he comments on the way both poems and snowshoes "hold us up," as if they are essential for our survival. He notes, in "Easter Maples" (p. 3), that "the pierced trees / pump their sweetness into pails," and mentally I make a connection with another tree pierced by iron nails, and the sweetness that continues to drip from it, like shed blood.

The intricately forested shorelines of Oregon, Washington and British Columbia are Loren's playground, his study, where his soul finds delight and meaning. Indeed, trees seem to be his special pleasure and symbol. He loves cedars. For him they seem to embody much of the natural world that is there for the seeing. He speaks in "That Tree Again" (p. 6) of the way an ancient tree falling in the deep forest is not real to us until we bushwhack our way in and stumble across it, echoing the old philosophical question: "If a tree falls in the forest and no one hears it, does it make a sound?"

In another favorite of mine, "Christmas, Whidbey Island, 1975" (p. 21) Loren speaks poignantly about the Incarnation of Christ as it shapes our thinking about the fleshy realities of our lives. In fact, if I were to characterize the whole opus I'd use the word "incarnational." Loren worships Christ as God in the flesh, and finds in the flesh of trees, rocks, rivers and friends these vivid images that find new shapes in his poetry.

Ever since reading these poems, beginning back in the '70s, I've longed for more of Loren, more of the unsensational, quiet life of an artist in the truest sense—one who "makes things"—constructing out of the earthiness of a fruitful life a rich humus for other life to feed on, grow and flourish. Including mine.

Luci Shaw
Bellingham, Washington

Author's Preface

These poems would never have been collected into this small book were it not for the persistent encouragement of my one-time student (from my first year at Regent, 1981), and long-time friend and colleague, Ron Reed. I am deeply grateful for that persistence; it has helped me overcome my long reluctance to publish this handful of poems.

That reluctance stems from two things. The first is that having been myself a teacher of "creative writing" for more than half a century, I am all too aware of how easy it is to overvalue one's work, and thus to be too eager to press it onto others for their approval and praise. Over those years of teaching, I have read a great deal of hopeful student poetry. I have tried hard to help these aspiring poets make their work better, and I think I have succeeded with some. But too often I have been tempted to agree with Flannery O'Connor's response when asked if she thought that the universities stifled would-be writers. Her reply: "I don't think they stifle enough of them." I would rather be silent than wished to be stifled.

Consequently, although I would like to believe that some of these poems are among the best and most important things I have written, I know how easy it is to be mistaken in such self-evaluation. So I have thought it better to be reticent about them.

The second reason for my reluctance to publish these poems is more troubling to me. It is simply the sad fact (sad at least to me) that the poems are so few in number, and so few are written recently. Many, perhaps most, of the best of them were written many years ago. Over the decades, I have managed to write on the average perhaps one poem a year. But to publish a book of poetry is (implicitly) to make the claim that "I am a poet." And I simply haven't written enough—especially in the 35 years since coming to Regent—to make that claim.

For a long time I comforted (or deluded) myself with the young Rainer Maria's Rilke's words in his autobiographical *The Notebooks of Malte Laurids Brigge*, about a young and unproductive writer: "Ah, but verses amount to so little when one writes them young. One ought to wait and gather sense and sweetness a whole life long, and a long life if possible. And then, quite at the end, one might perhaps be able to write ten lines that were good."

Rilke goes on to list the sort of experiences one must have—of joy, love, travel, and grief. Then he says that not till such experiences ". . . have turned to blood within us, to glance and gesture, nameless and no longer to be distinguished from ourselves--not till then can it happen that in a most rare hour the first word of a verse arises in their midst and goes forth from them."

Well, maybe. And I still hope for a time when (after the gift of already quite a long life), I might yet write at least "ten lines that [are] good"—as Rilke himself, after years of poetic near-silence, was blessed at the end of his life with the astonishing gift of the "Duino Elegies" and the "Sonnets to Orpheus." It is more likely though that the scarcity of these poems can be attributed more to laziness, busy-ness, and lack of discipline than to the lofty commitment to perfection which Rilke describes.

However, the great gift to me of Ron's commitment to shepherd these poems to publication is that it has, unexpectedly given me a perspective on the poems which makes me more favorably inclined both towards them, and the very full life out of which they have been written. Collecting and organizing them has helped me see that the poetry is perhaps part of a larger and more important task and story than the poems themselves.

In order to share this hopeful perspective I have to indulge in a little autobiography, and a little theology.

As several of the poems make clear, I was shaped by growing up near a forest along a river—the South Santiam—which drained the central Cascade mountains in Oregon. Among my earliest memories is wandering happily alone in that forest which my father, a last pioneer, was, with great effort, slowly reducing to fields. That childhood was my first introduction to the miracle of living, with open senses and a receptive mind, in this infinitely varied, beautiful, dangerous and surprising universe. Without thinking much about it, I knew that this gift I lived in was not merely "nature," but Creation: a gift indeed, of a Creator. That experience of growing up on that farm along the river was my first experience of Creation as a revelation about the meaning of things, a revelation which has never ceased to inspire me.

The second source of revelation, which also continues to shape and inspire me, was first absorbed from my family, a rural Sunday School (which was our only church), and various Christian camps. I grew up accepting (blessedly, without any significant period of rejection or rebellion) the Biblical and Christian account of what the Creator has been doing in history to make himself known more clearly. My understanding of that story has steadily deepened through the years.

Unfortunately, but not untypically, these two sources of revelation, in those early years, were never clearly connected to each other, though I was shaped thoroughly by both. And that apparent though illusory tension between the Creational revelation and the Christian revelation is really the main source of these poems. How is the word about Christ "in whom all things hold together" present in both Scripture and Creation? How does that presence of God in creation and in Jesus inform and shape our own presence in the world? Though the poems do many other things, they outline those questions by means of pieces of my own particular life in a particular place, among particular people.

The poems explore those questions not out of detached analysis, but rather out of the experience of living (as each of us does) a unique life, in a unique place, encountering unique creatures and persons. Art—the creative response to the wonder of creation—is the only way to communicate such experiences, which are basic to our humanity, giving rise to both worship and science.

But accompanying that initial response of wonder is our need to make things graspable and clear. In fact we have two essential, but often conflicting, ways of encountering the world: through empathetic wonder, and through clarifying simplification and explanation. As Iain McGilchrist has shown exhaustively in his great book, *The Master and His Emissary*, that seems to be the reason that we (along with birds and animals) have two halves to our brain. They are meant to work together, but always with the wondering, empathic and relational right hemisphere the master. All too often, however, the left hemisphere's itch for clarity and control usurps the master's role.

In a way these poems describe my encounter with those two revelations of God—in creation and Christ—in terms of that most primal and important way of knowing, through image and metaphor. One of McGilchrist's more revealing insights is that the left hemisphere, which is always trying to make things clear, for the good purposes of power and control, cannot by itself understand metaphor. Yet it is the right hemisphere's ability to encounter and name with metaphor the unique, the particular, and the new which continually revitalizes language and hands it back as a tool for the left hemisphere to use.

The pressures and expectations of scholarship and teaching, even in so rich an environment as Regent College, have been dominated by that left hemisphere's concern for clarity and simplification. This to me is borne out by the fact that for roughly 30 years I have been trying to write a book that makes explicit, in more analytic prose, some of the truths which I first discovered and expressed through the images and forms of poetry. And during that time, I haven't written much poetry.

The discipline of re-reading and organizing the poems for this book has made it clear to me that I have been working on the same project all along. In *Circles and the Cross* (the provisional title of that slowly-emerging book) I am trying to spell out truths I grasped in earlier poems. What does it mean (in terms of "Good Friday Up Milk Creek") that "in that sun's white, dying heart, / Abba, father, helium screams," and that "all things dying, sing"? What does it mean (in terms of "Christmas, Whidbey Island, 1975") that "if we stand in the straw of Bethlehem / Then God shines out from everything."? What does the "scandal of particularity" mean–that (in terms of "The Christ of Charlie Edenshaw") "God spoke here ["on this rain-blest coast"] in ravens' croak / Because "his maker's hands / Were nailed to other wood."? What does it mean (in terms of "Hot-Cross Buns") that in the cross of our body we stand "in the centre where all ways start"? What does it mean (in terms of "Gardener") that God "tends in each new Adam the garden of his earth"?

Preparation for this book has helped me to realize that in the poems I discovered and expressed for myself four truths, which I have been exploring in my teaching and other writing ever since, but usually in non-poetic forms. To express them non-poetically, these truths are:

1. That in our human creatureliness we are very much "dust of the earth" (and of the stars), sharing—in a way that the unfolding cosmological, evolutionary and ecological story dramatically demonstrates—the being, life, and even the rudimentary consciousness of all other creatures.

2. That the transcendent Creator who has been immanent in the cycles and the progression of this whole vast story has chosen to be immanent in a particular person, place and time in the man Jesus, whose life, meaning and person cannot be understood apart from the story of the Jews.

3. That the Incarnation of Jesus implies the event of the cross, and shows us that the, risk, suffering and vulnerability of the Creator lie at the center of all the cycles of Creation.

4. That to be *imago dei*, "in the image of God," implies the task and privilege of being also *imago mundi*, "image of the world," which we receive from God and are called to offer back as a thankful oblation: the gift of God's creation shaped and elevated by our own creativity. The central image of that oblation is perhaps gardening, but our offering encompasses what we eat, what we build, and all the ways that we nourish or diminish creation through our technology.

I do not regret my attempt to teach and write about these truths in prose, but I will be disappointed if, in these closing years of my life, that later writing does not sometimes shine with some of the metaphors of my earlier poetry.

Again, I am thankful to Ron for the occasion he has provided for me to see the unity of this life-long project, by urging that I publish these earlier poems as I continue to work on a very different sort of book. I am thankful also for his being such an enormously perceptive reader of the poems. The experience of working on this book has taught me things about myself and work in two stages: first (as I try to describe, above) through my own seeing the unity in the poems, and their connection with my other work; second, very recently, through reading Ron's own remarkably insightful analysis of the poems. I did not (at his request) read his detailed commentary till I had written most of this preface, but I am astonished and humbled by his insight and respect. Every writer should be blessed with such a reader!

A few notes in conclusion.

First, I do not mean, by this rather elaborate preface, to imply that all of the poems illustrate the four theological points made above, especially the more occasional and family-related poems in the last half of the book. But they are, I think, all informed by the vision I have tried to outline in those points.

In almost all cases, the poems are frankly autobiographical: the "I" of the poems is almost always me, with one very notable exception. In that (to me) unsettling poem, "Incarnicide," the "I" is someone else, perhaps the fallen Adam.

Finally: usually the "we" in the poems, implicit or explicit, involves my wife of 51 years, Mary Ruth. In only one poem ("The Sundays After Epiphany") is she mentioned directly by name, but her support through our long, very full life together is part of the life-blood of this book. The indirect reference to her in the sixth stanza of "Imago Mundi," through the great women who stand behind her name, is the closest I have yet come in the poems to expressing my love and gratitude for her.

In our time the virtual world seems to be crowding out the Creation which these poems celebrate. At the same time, in this "Anthropocene" age, the vitality of earthly Creation itself seems to be diminishing. Poetry seems very unimportant. But though I can perhaps agree with W. H. Auden's ironic lament that "poetry makes nothing happen," I deeply affirm the challenge to poets which closes the memorial to W. B. Yeats where those words appear:

> Follow, poet, follow right
> To the bottom of the night,
> With your unconstraining voice
> Still persuade us to rejoice;
>
> With the farming of a verse
> Make a vineyard of the curse,
> Sing of human unsuccess
> In a rapture of distress;
>
> In the deserts of the heart
> Let the healing fountain start,

Preface

In the prison of his days
Teach the free man how to praise.

I hope this very modest vineyard of verse can persuade
a few readers to both praise and rejoice.

Retreat Cove, Galiano Island
September, 2016

Introduction

Many have come to know Loren Wilkinson as a Regent College professor. An inspired and inspiring teacher, Loren invited students to accompany him on his explorations of the terrain where philosophy and theology interacts with the sciences and the arts, where the play of the imagination enlivens rational thought, where our interaction with the material and sensual world is complemented by thoughtful reflection and creative expression. At times these joint explorations were conducted in a classroom; more often, if at all possible, around a table. As far as Loren was concerned, the best setting was his home on Galiano Island, a ferry ride away from Vancouver, where the setting—natural, cultivated, built—informed and enriched these explorations of the whole person. The land and seascape became both context and focus for the explorations of these courses. Many lives have been transformed and enriched by being in the presence of Loren in his world: the dining room table, the garden, the seashore, boats, apple presses, cast-iron pans, books, chickens, trees, stones, driftwood and art works.

Fewer know that in one corner of this interdisciplinary terrain, this landscape of the embodied and engaged mind, Loren slowly built a body of poetry which, to introduce a new metaphor, provides a beautiful harmonic accompaniment to the melody of all that Loren has endeavoured to do as teacher, mentor and friend. The poems in this collection are an essential expression of a core belief which informs all of Loren's thinking; we are embodied creatures, embedded in the world (natural and cultural).

Living well involves grateful appreciation and honest engagement, loving God and his world with all our heart, mind, soul, strength, vulnerability, senses, and imagination. These poems are grounded in Loren's experience. There is dirt under the fingernails of the hand that wrote these lines, the particular dirt of the places where Loren has lived.

We live our lives in the interplay of opposites, beginning with our erect posture (the vertical) as we gaze and move forward (the horizontal). Our bilateral symmetry is the foundation and matrix of the many opposites we experience: the real and the imaginary; reason and imagination/emotion; mind and body, or mind and matter; and the natural and human worlds (creation and culture).

While our world (and how we experience it) is characterized by opposites, we have both opportunity and ability to seek integration and wholeness, to perceive unity, to hear the rich harmonics that arise out of the oppositional dichotomies.

It can be argued that all good art serves this reaching for integration, which is seen in two of Loren's Easter poems, "Easter Maples" and "Easter Eggs." While each stands alone, something new emerges when they are read together. One poem is set in the natural world (trees, weather, earth, water, and birds, with only the unnamed man driving nails to hang pails), while the other lists mostly human-made things and surroundings (cellophane sacks, plastic, rooms, chairs, cushions). What connects the two is the sweetness of trees and singing birds, representing the resurrection life of Easter. Think of the two poems as dual speakers emitting the stereo sounds of Easter's promise.

Another Easter poem in the collection, "Gardener," has to do with different opposites. Mary mistakes the identity of the gardener; Loren makes us aware of a deeper misidentification. The risen Christ is indeed a gardener, a second Adam, tending and redeeming the garden of the whole world. More than that, a new identity is revealed: gardener and garden are really one.

Loren understands that there are profound truths which require the language of myth and is aware of the tensions between mythic truth and gospel truth. Another poem, "The Christ of Charlie Edenshaw," goes a long way to articulate this tension while overcoming it and allowing us to hear new resulting harmonies in the process.

The relationship between humanity and the rest of nature is often perceived and portrayed in confrontational terms. Nature is something to be controlled, overcome, maybe feared, perhaps protected. Think of weeds, wolves, winter, wheat, white-water, wilderness. "Gardener" suggests a different vision, a unity or a correspondence between ourselves and the natural world.

Introduction

In "The Honeymoon Mine" Loren develops this theme in a different direction. The prospector, who is at first the impatient, resentful conqueror of nature, begins to experience (albeit mostly subconsciously) a correspondence between his body and the mountain of his obsession, awakening in him other desires. The wife he acquires is treated the same way as the rock, and in the end both fail him as he has failed himself. The portrait and narrative of this poem portray a profound misunderstanding or misappropriation of the truth and promise of Easter, the promised unity gone awry.

Other oppositions found in these poems are life and death, the universal and the particular, the extraordinary found in the ordinary, music and dance in contrast to the spoken word, the interplay of Christmas (Incarnation) with Good Friday and Easter.

There is a constant ground—a bass/continuo, if you like—that undergirds the play of themes and forms (melodies and harmonies) of these poems, the recognition and acknowledgement of being part of a grand narrative that reaches back to Eden and forward to a "new heaven and earth" ("The Seal"). It is a story carried forward by God's ongoing creation and redemptive recreation, and by our participation: through the work of our hands and the "work of the people" (liturgy), in the cycles and rhythms of our days and years, and in the ongoing challenge and opportunity to find and make wholeness out of the oppositions and dichotomies of our lives.

Rudi Krause

"Man is the priest of a cosmic sacrament, receiving the world from God and offering it back to God in thankfulness."
—Alexander Schmemann, *For the Life of the World*

EDEN'S LEAVES

Eden's leaves
Hide lost beasts:
Lion's song,
Hawk's speech:

Under leaves
In violet light
Weaves and trembles
Eve's fright.

For Eve deceived
Ate fruit of the moon
On steep trees
In the first noon

And beasts are dumb
In violent light
And thistles come
In the long night

And Adam's eyes
Are strange and cold
And Eve's face
Is white and old.

Now Eve leaves
Old graces
For dry weeds
Waste places:

Beasts bleed
In the wild place
And Eve seeks
Her lost face.

EASTER MAPLES

I

The thin geometries of maple trees
Freeze in the sleet.
But the roots slant down
Between the limestone and the frost
And know, in the dark of their death,
When to live.

II

Hardly breaking the crust on the snow
The man drives hollow nails
Till iron echoes in the gray grove
And branches of the frozen trees
Rattle in a February wind.

III

All day, dripping in the woods,
The pierced trees
   Pump their sweetness into pails.
Above, among the buds,
A scarlet bird
Sings water down the streams.

Warmed under wings of unholy ghosts,
On Holy Saturday the candy eggs
Hatch and holler "buy me"!
From their cellophane sacks.

And in the night the children sleep
Tucked in plastic beds
With candy ducks in plastic grass
Quacking in their heads.

But in the April dawn
They enter the cool light of living rooms
Where color blooms in the corners.
Green beneath the chairs, scarlet in the cushions,
In its shadows the room hides sweetness like a tree.

For an instant the children wait surprised,
As women in an unexpected spring might wait
Before trilliums, and the singing birds,
And the emptiness of tombs.

THE NECESSITY OF SNOWSHOES
(for Robert Frost)

Twigs talk in the wind there;
Snow piles script on limbs of an oak.
Indeed, the woods are lovely,

But if you leave the road
You'll sink, crotch-deep,
In downy flakes gone mad with multitude.

We are too pointed for deep snow;
Our heavy feet plunge postholes in the stuff.
Without the secret feet of hares,
The lightness of a quail,
We flounder belly-deep like deer.

So cut an ash no thicker than your wrist,
Shave the outer wood away and bend it to a frame.
Lace the frame with rawhide, wet
(Slippery as worms, or words).
Draw it tight and let it dry,
A hide-hard latticework of stars.

Then walk as lightly as a fox.
Those careful shapes will hold you up
Like poems on the world's white wilderness,
And give you paths around the rocks
To snow-cliffs that the stream cuts deep,
Or quiet places under pines
And large simplicities of sleep.

…falling always in the soundless wood,
with no eyes watching from the brush,
no ears to hear the great limbs split
and splinter into always-fertile earth,
so far away the echo does not reach us,
not even the most distant of thunders,

and we did not see it before,
nor shall not find it after:
it falls in the secret place
at the center of all woods
where deer doze all day long in the shade,
and trilliums open trinities of white,

beside the stream that pours across a log
from nowhere into nowhere,
through a place we cannot find,
where wood ducks, bright as clowns,
nest in hollow trees above the spring,
in the shadow of that tree, still falling,

always in the soundless wood,
outside all minds in a place we cannot reach,
which we are imagining,
where the great tree stands rooted still
above the trilliums and the sleeping deer,
and will not fall till we arrive.

THE HONEYMOON MINE

I

A rootless man with treasure in his head,
He stumbled through the woods
And tripped on roots
And cursed the rock-obscuring bounty of the rain:
The moss, the mud, the dripping ferns,
The trees that rooted in the rock
And split it with their growth--
He willed them all away.

He wanted rock alone
And scraped the forest's muck
In search of it:
Galena's gleam,
Or glitter of the gold-flecked quartz,
Or green sheen of the malachite.
He wanted hidden things laid bare
And blundering through the woods
He watched for them
Thrusting to the surface in the earth's slow pulse.

II

One spring he burrowed through the brush
To the base of a peak that pushed
Three stone fingers into nothing.
Water poured from the rock,
Dripped from the roots
And stripped the dirt away from stone.

He saw the black rock glitter in the spray,
Saw the white rock glitter in the black,
And dreamed of tracing back that vein
To treasure at the mountain's core.

All summer long
With pick and drill and dynamite
He dug beneath the waterfall,
Poking one long empty thumb
Into the mountain's side.
But as the rich rock broke beneath his pick,
The sound of water dripping,
Dripping down the roots
Outside the mine
Tunnelled in his mind,
Echoed in the tunnel
And haunted his dark with images of life:
Cedar-smell, and ferns like girls' hair;
Salal leaves smooth as flesh,
And blueberries crushed into juice
On his rockdust-covered tongue.

III

That fall, sound of water in his ears
He built a cabin:
Roofed with cedar,
Bolted to the rock,
He waited out the pressure of the snow
And in the spring
He went to town and got a wife.

That night, floods poured off the rock.
By light of candles from the mine
He stripped her in the flickering loft,
Touched her thighs with hands like stone
And in the dark of her breasts
Rode the roar of the waterfall
Deeper to the peak's stone core
Than his mine could ever thrust.

IV

The vein played out by summer's end.
The girl left by Christmas,
Scared out by his stony hands,
His anger at the rock.

But the cabin is there still,
Collapsing down to humus
Around an iron bed.
His hole in the rock
Is good as new:
You can stumble up it now
To its fool's gold end
And look back out
At silver drops
Dripping
Dripping
From the
Green
Fern's
Root.

GOOD FRIDAY, UP MILK CREEK

In the hanging valley of Milk Creek
Skunk cabbage flares at dusk
In yellow tongues above the mud
And cedars lift past last year's leaves
Beat bloodless by the snow
And white as children's hands.

All night the high snows melt
Their water down the rock
And shape its veins and diorite
In curves like stretching flesh.
In withered ferns a sleeping man
Dreams along his bones
The long and artless elegy
That water sings to stone.

The river resurrects the ferns;
The sun surmounts the ridge.
Past cedars whorled like nebulae,
It casts an avalanche of light
Against the valley's side.

Back in that sun's white dying heart,
Abba, Father, helium screams
And bleeds its heat down on this hill
Where lichens leach the stone away
The stone gives up its atoms to the soil,
The soil its strength to roots,
Whose flowers hollow wombs beneath the snow
And then break out like flame.

Light fallen from a dying star
Warms fingerflesh on stone
And from its cleft the bleeding-heart
Drops color on the moss.
Leaf takes its green from granite,
Thing gives life to thing;
Flesh takes its blood from sun
And all things, dying, sing.

THREE WAYS OF FACING A STORM

I Jellyfish

Their flesh is frail as comet's tails
And beats the fertile billows
Through the plasmas of their gut.
The ocean is their body and their blood.
The ocean is their will.
At peace with everything,
They go where currents go:
In tidal waves or hurricanes
They drift their hungry gauze
And after storms die glinting on the beach
In crystalline collapse.

II Jonah

His will at peace with nothing,
He sleeps an oaken inch from waves
Vexed for him to madness.
No shipboard gods will calm them,
And men with terror in their eyes
Drag him to the deck
And pitch him in the sea.
The great fish takes him like a tomb,
And in the evening's calm
The quiet sailors
Tidy up their ship
In terror of his God.

III Jesus

He also sleeps within the boat
(His sea-salt blood,his mammal's flesh)
With fishscales in his hair.
The storm comes up so fast
Even the fishermen are scared.
Wind's waves will not wake him;
Their yells do.
"Peace, sea," he speaks:
And calm spreads out
Across the lake, the men,
Like dawn in empty tombs.

WITCHING
(a poem for Grandpa)

Behind the barn we scuffed
Across the cowpies and the quartz
My back against his thighs,
His hands on mine, and mine gripped tight
Upon a slick-peeled hazel Y.

Erect before us both, it led.
He said, "That wand is water-wise.
Its lopped-off roots have left
Their longings in the wood,
And so it points to pools below the dirt."

His zeal embarassed me.
He smelled like oil and old sheep
And his gadget-happy hands
Were stones upon my own.
But sure enough:

Before we'd paced ten steps
The wise white root flipped down
And quivered like a sapling at the ground.
"Water there in 20 feet." he said,
But neither of us dug that well.

My daddy dug a grave instead
Where grandpa's hands can flourish in the dirt
Like hazels sending roots in search of rain,
Like his own root delved daddy and myself
From the well of grandma's womb.

BAPTISM

After church
We drove backroads to the river
Past boysenberries, plum trees
And an old John Deere
Disc-deep in clods
And cold as a troll
Where Sunday caught it.

We came down to the water
Where dinner was laid
Potluck and without price
On old planks.
I ate jello and baked beans
And watched the rest skip stones
Across the unyielding water.

After dinner I waded out,
White-shirted,
Scared to death of water,
Embarassed by the act,
But wanting it,
To let the preacher shove me under
In the name of a
Half-known trinity.

    (The Santiam is clear there,
    Five miles below the farm,
    And colder, joined a mile upstream
    By the North fork

Whose tributaries drain
The great white throne
Of glaciers)

I rose up spluttering
And stumbled over lucid stones
Back to the waiting shore where
The brisk breeze shivered me.

Downstream, a heron flapped up
Past ancient cottonwoods,
Rooted deep, like myself,
And green with the water's life.

IN WINTER'S WET IN OREGON

In winter's wet in Oregon
The rafters ripened in the dark
And nightly built around my dreams
A skull of fir stumps
Rotting in the rain.

The winter-heavy river
Roared beyond the woods
Whose trees came back at night
To crowd with squawking nests
Against my sleep.

Herons gibbered in my dreams,
And under squabbles over fish
The river shifted pebbles to the sea.
Among the hungry birds I slept
Above the marshes and the brush

Till morning, and the drip
Of spent rain on the shakes:
And the spit and snap of fire
Growing from the kindling
Of my father's hands.

The bloom of carcinoma in his bones
Brought forth its fruit when stubble fields were burned.
The cottonwood and maple trees had turned.
Along the Santiam the sunburnt stones
Were lucent, lucid underneath the flow
Cascading from fall showers in the hills.
Blue herons stood and dipped their bills
For fattened fish; the whirlpools were slow.

The ocean drew its river like a tide.

Beside that sea I watched the water run
Out and out. The night my father died
The tide went low; the crescent moon was done.
I watched across the peaks its bright horn glide
Like some great beast running, running toward the sun.

CARNELIAN

The creek that crooked its elbow round our farm
Dug with rainy fingers in the hills
And bumped its boulders yearly toward the sea.

In flood, it flowed across the fields;
In summer, gravel bars exposed,
It drained through drifts of colored stones.

One August, on a blazing day
We stopped the chainsaw and the cat
And stumped across the bleaching rocks

And stripped and stepped into the cold
That thrust between warm shallows
At the center of the flow.

The sun embarrassed daddy's flesh, and mine:
I looked away and waded deeper in,
Clothed me with the current's cool.

Afterwards, walking back to work
(Shadows cooler, hair wet on my neck)
We looked for rocks along the bar.

He found an agate, bigger than his fist,
Banded, pink and clear like flesh
fresh-cut, too pained to bleed.

"That there's carnelian," he said.
(I knew from Sunday school)
Those gems formed heaven's walls

And later learned
(Ages from such stones)
Carnelian meant flesh.

In summers now I walk those rocks alone.
Heat beats upward
From the river-rolled basalt

And I squint and scrabble
In the flood-dug rubble of these hills
For the chunk of red carnelian
That holds my father's heart.

CHRISTMAS, WHIDBEY ISLAND, 1975

Not in the waves, nor in the wave-torn kelp;
Not in the heron by the lake at dawn,
Nor owls' haunting of the wood,
Nor rabbits browsing frightened on the lawn;
Neither in the widening whirl
Of seashell, galaxy, or cedar burl,
Nor in the mushrooms' bursting of the humid ground:
In nothing of his bright, shy world
May God the fathering be found,

If not found first in Bethlehem,
In thistly hay, on hoof-packed earth,
Where a girl, cruciform with pain
Grips manger boards in childbirth.
There in the harsh particular,
In drafts and stench of cow manure,
The squawls of Christ, creator, sound:
Where God grasped not at Godhead in a child,
There only will the God of life be found.

Now: if we upon this wave-shaped bluff
Stand in the straw of Bethlehem
Then God shines out from everything:
The agate in the surf, the withered flower stem,
The fish that gives its body for the seal,
The flesh, the fruits that form each common meal,
The dance of pain and love in which our lives are wound:
Since God was flesh at Bethlehem,
In all the world's flesh may God be found.

21

THE CHRIST OF CHARLIE EDENSHAW
(for Roy Vickers)

Dawn-bringer:
Raven,
Who let there be light.

Shape-changer:
Raven,
Color of night.

Man-maker:
Raven,
Who sets things right.

I

In the smoky lodge at night, they knew
(Tlingit, Chilkat, Haida);
On the beach at dawn, they knew
(Tsimshan, Kwakiutl, Makah);
In the dripping cedar woods, they knew
(Bella Coola, Salish, Nootka)
That Raven, who found man in a mussel shell,
That Raven, Raven is the bringer of the light.

II

Raven's children loved the touch of things:
Opalescent abalone,
Winking from a bear's carved head;
Argilite, like ebony.
Goat's wool,

22

Seal-skin,
Spruce-root, twisted into cord:
The glory of the thing—

But most of all, the cedar:
Raven gave them cedar
and taught them how to carve,
To wake the full-fleshed forms
Within the incense of the tree:
How eagle, whale, mosquito, bear,
Beaver, deer and man
Made one long dance of chiselled flesh
Within the living wood.

Raven taught the sacrament
Of the half-guessed, thousand-fleshed god
Whose own hands carved the earth:
And in front of the lodge in sunlight,
Beneath strong fingers,
Shavings curled away
Till what remained
Was wood made live again
With raven's life, maker's life.

III

When Jesus was born in Judea
Here, between the cedars and the tide,
Old men already carved God's words
In shapes like ravens' eyes,

And waited, on this rain-blest coast,
For light-bringer, raven,

Blackened in the smoke-hole trap,
To spread white wings again:

To brood within the shaper's heart.
The shaper's touch, half understood,
What God spoke here in ravens' croak
Because his maker's hands
Were nailed to other wood.

BEACH DREAM
(at Ozette, Washington)

The old ones wove their capes of shredded cedar
Stripped in spring from trees by forest-walkers,
Coiled and carried back near sound of waves
By women happy at the end of winter,
Who sat in sun among the drift
And watched the wading of the herons.

We still watch solitary herons
From logs that then were living cedar,
And stretch our bones among the ancient drift,
Or watch the nylon-sheltered walkers
Who praise the passing of the winter
And pace beneath their packs along the waves,

Where those who lived here walked by other waves,
That hissed like these around the legs of herons,
Or burst past tops of islands in the winter
When all that stopped the storm was cedar,
Split in planks by forest-walkers
And raised in walls behind the wave-wrecked drift.

We shiver in this sudden-shadowed drift,
Remembering the thousand years' of waves,
The years and tears of rain-soaked walkers,
The surf too swift and cold for herons,
That dug and drowned this once-young cedar
And left it here within the old-ones winter.

They faced such storms for winter after winter.
We dream them, on those winter seas adrift,
In long canoes shell-adzed from straight-grained cedar,
Awash with cold and ever-cresting waves,
Too far out from rocks that shelter herons
And sands where stand the ever-watching walkers.

But we, these rain-proof, land-bound walkers
Wake from this dream of drizzling winter
To this warm seascape, blessed by herons
And gulls that peck among the fertile drift,
To trace the foam of broken waves,
Or whittle on a stick of sea-shaped cedar:

For every walker waits to rest his bones in drift:
To dream no more of winter on the waves,
But watch the herons from the shelter of the cedar.

FOR THE WOMAN WHO DIED IN THE LOUNGE AT OLD FAITHFUL INN

That morning, when you drove into the park,
A great elk grazed beside its traffic jam;
You wondered how a beast as big as that
Could be so tame.

At noon, beneath a polaroid sky,
You posed beneath the poised plume
And wished that all your grandchildren
Could be here now.

All afternoon you walked through steam
By geysers, mudpots, fumaroles
And asked your husband if this heat
Could ever cool.

Toward evening, when you peered into a pool
That funnelled blue through andesite
You saw the troubled waters bulge
But did not move.

After supper, sitting on a rustic chair,
You felt, through andesites of pain
The geysers of your blood go up
And could not move.

    We stood on wooden balconies
    And watched them seek your pulse an hour.
    Outside, above the drifting steam,
    The cold moon rose.

GARDENER

When Mary Magdalene
Saw Christ at dawn
In the tomb-haunted grove
She thought he was the gardener,
Then saw He was the Christ

But still she was mistaken,
Not seeing that
The flowers in the rock
The grass
The gnarled, deep-rooted olive trees
The rock itself
Were rooted in his flesh
And nourished by his fresh-shed blood.

For Christ was gardener of that place
But hid his workman's hands,
The flowers of his flesh,
Lest the young church see
Persephone,
Osiris,
Gaia,
Or only wild Pan,
And not the God beyond the world
Who made it
For our flesh
And His
And tends, in each new Adam,
The garden of His earth.

THE GREEN SPRINGS
(Lincoln, Oregon, Easter, 1981)

These mountains too are places of a cross.
Moss grows on dumps and logging ruts,
On cuts and stumps of deep-eroded slopes,
On hopes for profit, skeletons of loss.

On Soda Mountain, Chinquapin, on Hobart's Bluff,
Rough, the wind pours rain against the hills,
Spills down ledges, gullies, rotted logs,
Slogs winterfulls of water onto forest duff.

Sink then into dirt and die, rain:
Drain through mud and lava dust, descend:
End your kenosis in a sheol of basalt
Faulted, broken with the planet's pain.

Seep deep along the ancient flaws: leach,
Preach in a hell of dusty stones.
Bones will break out with flesh,
Fresh as manzanita twigs that rise, reach

Blossom in an April dawn.
On hillsides crucified, spring!
Sing life to trilliums, camas, watercress,
Press sap through stems and cascade on

Past bulbs and roots and rhizomes; stream
To Keene Creek, and the Klamath, and the sea
As we turn cityward to leave,
Grieve, grow, leaf skeletons with green.

INCARNICIDE

The great grey alder limbs arch over to the river's shore
And here I was alone all day with my world and my words:
You did not come from the cedar-scented wood,
Nor from the river, nor the gull-blessed, beckoning sea,
You did not come at all. But out from bushes came the hare,
The otter from the ferns, the serpent from his hole beneath
the stone.

In the shadow of my namer I named them all alone
Till after river-brightened dusk there were no more
Except the alder at my back, muscular and bare
And branched in limbs above me through the silence
of the birds.
The earth was fertile in the dark, and I slept beside the tree
Where your singing woke me, and I thought I understood:

That river, otter, alder…all created things were good
If you were flesh with my flesh, you were bone with bone:
So we shaped the world together in the song you sang to me
And we grew like gods together from our godlike core,
Till the beasts that fled before us were raucous and absurd
In the shining of our godlike stare.

Long since, we left the river for a steep and muddy stair
That led us nameless, to a city made of wood
Where your song grew thick with solipsy and surds
And led us to a city made of stone
Where I pierced you to your sick heart's core
And dragged your bleeding body to this river by the sea
And scooped a grave from silt beneath this alder tree,

Shoveled muck back over your eyes, your thighs, your hair,
Which will twist my life no longer: you will name my
world no more.
Beneath these dripping limbs, in lifeless mud, I now
have stood
For hours, by your buried flesh alone.
No creatures rustle in the bush. There are not any birds.

But whispers, only, of the waiting namer's words:
That he waits within the wood to give a name to me:
That he lived within such skin, died within such bone
And only in such shivering flesh can bear
Her murder for my everlasting good:
And that her grave is his beside this alder-arching shore.

The words have left her buried, and they leave the gray
limbs bare,
But they beckon like the river-drawing sea: as after death
he stood
Alive by empty stone, so might her body blossom
by this shore.

WRECK BEACH, VANCOUVER

All day behind the tinted glass,
The rust-resistant steel,
On polyester rugs the people pass or pause
And feel the susurration of the air
Through miles of metal ducts,
Feel flush and pulse of their own blood
Beneath their covered skin,
Feel skin beneath the bands
And bags and billows
Of their clothes:

So, male and female,
They pass into the sun,
Into the wind from cedar and salal,
Shedding nylon, polyester, steel,
Down to the lost Eden of the beach,
Strip to the innocence of skin,
Match curve of hip to alder curve,
Press thighs against the flesh-shaped stone
By rippled, nippled sand,

And I watch in zippered horror from the cedar and salal.
What was the wreck that doomed their sun-flecked nudity?
Is the sinning in my eyes, or in their skin?
Is the Fall in the sun-flushed flesh of their loins
Where they sprawl between the Eden of the alders
And the calling of the tide,
Or does it rise behind my eyes,
Erect and unsurprised

From a pit as old as Hell?
I cannot blame the hormone's spell.
I know the answer very well.

WEDDING IN OCTOBER
(for Sherri and David Koster)

What does it mean, in Alberta, in October,
That we wait here between the birches and the river
And watch these two pledge faithfulness forever?

      Right now the sun is warm above the clouds;
      Last night the frost was deep.
      All things wear out, and winter comes:

      Geese breed, and feed, then flee the darkening north
      (This dawn the sky
      Was clamorous with their south-bound cries.)

      Not even larch are evergreen.
      Like birch they flare, then flame, then wither in the frost,
      And men kick dreams about their feet as thick as as-
      pen leaves.

      Weddings wither also. Vows break like brittle leaves.
      So what does it mean that these two
      Now, not in the green juice of June,

      But in October, after frost, in the chilling death of the year
      Stand up above a yet-unfrozen stream
      To make their marriage live?

Listen: you who wait with them here
In the bare birch wood at the beginning of winter:
Not all vows break.

Two nights ago, driving from the West,
We stopped by another river, running seaward,
Down the mountains from the river and the ice.

Flowing in the cedar woods, it was thick with salmon:
Gray in the starlight, bodies filled with promises,
They swam all night against the stream.

We watched them fling their weight across the stones
To keep a pledge made in their flesh,
That after ice, their young would reach the sea.

And shall these two not keep their pledge
Made both in spirit and in flesh
To swim against the current of these times,

And build with love a home as strong
As mortised cedars build this house
By which we watch them make their autumn vows?

For they are built together in one whose own vows never broke:
Christ, who broke his body for this dying world 's life,
As they give soul and body as a husband, as a wife.

Warburg, Alberta

COMMUNION IN VANCOUVER

I

Blessed with flesh,
We thresh in the terror of death:
Bad dreams twist us
In the loins,
In the head
And each seeks dippersfull of joy
From the dry hole
Of a well dug down to bedrock.

We do not presume to come to this thy table, O merciful Lord,
Trusting in our own righteousness, but in thy manifold and great
mercies. . . .

II

On an icy Sunday morning
At the corner of Cartier and Nanton
A silver-haired woman, going to church
Slipped in the cross of the road
And struggled on her back to rise
Till (one on her right and one on her left)
Two women helped her in to church.
Blood matted in her hair,
And in the fox-fur of her coat:
At the crossing where she lay
Bright drops cooled on the ice.

The Body of our Lord Jesus Christ, which was given for thee,
preserve thy body and soul unto everlasting life.

And now on Sunday our God rains,
Rains here in this rain-washed pleasure-dome of a city:
Rains in torrents on the wrack and wreck of a winter beach,
At the river's mouth, where herons wade
And old logs rot on the sandy mud.
Still falls the rain:
On empty gardens,
On cedar stumps,
On the gray tile roof
Of St. John's Shaughnessy,
Where now on a gray day
By rainlight
People make their way
To the way which is not their way:
Kneeling under narrow windows
Pieced together
From broken
Old stained glass,
Kneeling to take
A bit of bread,
A sip of wine
Beneath the concrete arches
Of St. John's Shaughnessy.

*Drink this in remembrance that Christ's blood was shed for thee,
and be thankful.*

IV

The narrow windows by the altar
Are made of broken glass

Blown eight hundred years ago
From a molten, brilliant mass
In Canterbury:

And all those centuries
In shapes of saints and angels
The bright glass stained the light
In the church where Thomas Becket
Was murdered by the king.

Till forty years ago,
In the Battle of Britain
The planes keened in from the French coast
And dropped their bombs
And were gone:

In the church at dawn
A woman found the shards,
The broken shapes,
Gleaming like blood and sapphire
On the icy stone,

And gleaned the glass
Which came at last to this place
Where it brightens rainlight
Shed on the wine, onthe bread
Of communion in Vancouver.

O Lamb of God, that takest away the sin of the world, have mercy upon us.

V

The broad arched window on the south side of the church
Blesses a soldier, a sailor, a pilot, and a nurse,
Who kneels on pale-green grass, her arm around a lamb.
The soldier prays: his rifle points at the earth.

O Lamb of God, that takest away the sin of the world, have mercy
upon us.

VI

O Vancouver, Vancouver,
(West End, Kerrisdale, Shaugnessy)
Not one stone will be left upon another:
For the bombs are already aimed
(Staying their fervent heat
For yet a little while).

Perhaps, after the blast,
The shock, the firestorm,
These concrete arches still will stand
Beneath their blackened cross
As a burnt dome stood
At Hiroshima

But the Canterbury glass
Will have shattered one last time:
On the north from the harbor bomb
On the south from the blasts
At the Trident base in its quiet place
On Puget Sound,
And the ancient blood-red glass
Will melt again and flow like blood;

The molten silver candlesticks
Will drip like rain
Where now the people kneel, at communion
In Vancouver.

O Lamb of God, that takest away the sin of the world, grant us thy peace.

Lent
Vancouver, 1985

DONOR

(for the guitarist's son, with leukemia)

The first part of the treatment
    is the chemical searing
    of the marrow of your bone

The next part is a bath
    of gamma rays
    that with the light touch

Of nuclear decay
    unmakes (perhaps)
    the clinging virulence

Of death
    in your inmost part.
    until you are in every way

As close to death
    as flesh and bone might come
    and still bear blood.

And as your father
    plucked you from curves
    of your mother's flesh

He now plucks
    from the taut strings of the guitar
    the pattern of Bach's lute suite No. 3

Which is
   the image of heaven,
   and health:

The deeper dance
   your blood and bone
   requires.

Below brown bluffs
Ebey's lagoon
Lay landlooped, rock-locked
Silting tidelessly and long
Behind the white-log tumble
Of its tide-scooped gravel spit
Where we sat, years-past, and watched the spring sun slide
Toward the oceanic origin of the inward-roaring tide.

Above silt flats
Flies bit.
When we dug that muck
The smell was rot and sulphur.
Nothing would live in that brown water;
No kingfisher fished in the shallows.
But west, the long waves pulled, and in the pebble-rush of lulls
We heard the chirp of scoter and the laugh of herring gulls.

All that
Was years ago
And we who watched waves then,
Backs to that brown pond,
(Like drift in the brackish shallows)
Were scattered, silt-fast, salt-stained
Walled each in his own disconsolancy
From the always-falling waves of the ever-rising sea.

And only two
Came down at dusk

From the windswept bluff
Past wild violets in the grass
To find the dead lagoon not brown
But fresh and flooding with the tide
In a swift stream sliced through the driftwood bones
Where an unwatched storm had moved those stones.

Long-settled silt
Was rinsed to sand
And a great blue heron
Waded after minnows.
Scoter skittered toward us
In a spume of sunlit spray
And a bright fish leaped from the bay's bright face
As though it had just come from some deep place.

Whidbey Island, 1984

CELLO CONCERTO

I dreamed that men and women
Walled up in the hollow place of their soul
Could utter only shallow things
Across the space that sundered
Each from all.

And because their hands were quicker
Than their slowly-spoken selves
I dreamed they crafted brass
And rosewood, ebony and wire
As voices for their soul:

The cords of their throat
Were not enough:
But with these strange-shaped extras to their flesh
(Viola, cello, trumpet, drum)
All things could now be said.

The walled-up hollows woke and spoke:
The taut wires now
Were urgent nerves
And from each wood and metal mouth
Empty places sang and wept

And I no longer slept.

NIGHTPATHS

(Variations on a theme by John Fowles)

Sometimes at night when I read
The patterns of print crumble and erode
Beneath the twigs and tendrils of a wood:
That Birnam wood, that Beauty's briar
Which always crowds the clearing of my thought
But nightly widens into wilds.

Then shedding book, clothes, mind, self
I slip back down my blood and sleep:
To run till dawn in the world's wide wood,
Sink fingers in the rot of leaves
Or trace a trickle to its source
And drink from undiscovered springs.

At waking, I step from the trees,
Shake leaf-dust from my eyes
And watch the shadows shorten
On the clearings of the world:
Architecture, pavement, print,
All day I walk those lines with care

Till sleep and trees
Stretch out their limbs again.

IMAGO MUNDI

I

Cast from sleep on the edge of a March dawn
(Brain as empty as a beach
The arch above our bed dark as the firmament)
We lie and listen to the birds
Seeking in the garden outside the glass:
    "Light, Light, who let there be light?"
    "We are glad for the light and the worms in the grass."
But it was only we who heard their chirp as words:
Their praise was wordless as their wonderment;
Our task was still like Eve's and Adam's all day long
To speak the light of language to the universe.

II

The late light flakes blown by the dawn wind
In the garden are stars of ice and air and sparkle
In the dark-branched shrub of my lung.
In alveolar lace there iron rusts and rushes
Blood-borne to my body's billion fires
Whose fuel is the heavy ash of stars,
Scattered from the novae of their pyres:
Carbon, and the ferrous rust that pushes
Wordless blood to my unbound tongue
To praise: that the God of the cosmos
Let the heavens come to speech in me.

III

Pouring from the west the sea-wind batters the town,
Strews branches like the wrack of tides

And warms the land with sea-smell.
The sea beats louder through the salt of my blood,
Whispers in my pink bones basinning basalt.
 O You who wove me in the depths of earth and ocean,
Who at the birth of light and stars foresaw the far result
Of the wind of your spirit quickening my mud:
Let deeps of sea and continent rise up in me and tell
That the whispering in the earthquake and the surf
Is the shout of your life in us who are water and dust.

IV

Standing on the thrusting grass by the choked pear-tree
The gnarled gardener is older than the trunk he tends.
The tendrils of the weed he strips from the limb
Have wrapped round both its twigs and his
And link the laddered acid of his seed
Back down to planet and to plant.
His fingers tend the garden's need:
Yet the transpired breath of the garden is
The respired breath of his work, which is the hymn
Of his soul and the grown voice of the soil rejoicing:
That dropped and rotting seeds may blossom yet from the dirt.

V

Now in the darkening afternoon
The animals watch from the garden's verge,
Shaped like versions of myself in the forests of my sleep
(Though I wake to kill them and eat).
Caught by their horns in our thickets they thresh
To escape us, the birds and the beasts.
And still through the ripped veils of their flesh
We enter with trampling feet

The violent sanctum of our unkept Keep:
And no slain lamb or ram nor any blood of bull or dove
Can give back the peace of our lost first task.

VI

Image of God, we say, and image of the world:
Eve, sorrowing, and blest-for-all-of-mankind, Mary
(Ruth-like in the fields, hopeful in the reaped wheat
To glean the grace of her promised pain),
And Jesus, like a mother at the town's dark side
Stretched with pain of making, and of making Man,
Who taught us how to be crucified
(We who would rather be slayers than slain);
He whom the Magdalene only could greet
At first as the gardener: Exactly the image of God--
Christ, who returned us the gardener's task.

VII

Creation waits now for the gardener to speak:
And the eager weeds await their release
From the bondage of being weeds.
Eden and Zion lie far apart
But atom and ocean, beasts and plants
Wait for the one who will grant them peace.
Then the planet will spin in a sabbath dance
(And the dancing place will be the heart).
Fruit will burgeon from scattered seeds
And garden and town be clean as a fleece
Early in the morning, on the first day of the week.

Selwyn Gardens, Cambridge
Holy Week, 1986

12 months past
On the morning
Of Good Friday
Past daffodils
In rain-light,
Before the day's traffic woke the town,
Through Newnham Garden to Newnham Croft
I walked down aisles of bursting willow
And alleys by houses of weathered stone
To the fragrant, shuttered bakery shop:

To buy a dozen
Buns, hot (cut
With a cross &
Round as time)
For my family.

(This solstice
Again, violets
Push and splay
And deep trees
All luxuriate:
Their roots reach out in soil and time
Past Roman, Saxon, Norman bones placed
Past standing, horizontal under stone;
The rains pour down; the trees grow up
Round and round in the season's cycle.

The year turns
And it returns
Wet time; dry;
Cold time; hot
Bright, dark.)

The baker shop
In chilly dawn
Pulled people
Like a centre
From the town:
Old women, and men, like trees walking
And one who spread arms to his child,
In body's shape, the shape of a cross:
This upward axis, from earth to heaven,
This outward axis through which we act.
This hot bread
Holds the crux,
This centre in
The cycle where
All ways start.

Cambridge, 1986;
Vancouver, 1987

BURNING THE CHRISTMAS TREE

February, and time to burn the Christmas tree
(Dropping needles in its desolate corner).
In December, already dying, it hinted still
Of green wilderness, and we hung our family's past
On its resinous bounty:

(Noriko's origami stars; Judy's sheep;
From Whidbey Island, Andy's painted pins;
Crocheted snowflakes from Lola on the Greensprings,
And Bruce and Robin's lion and lamb,
Still peaceful in their play-dough wreath.)

But now not even the coloured lights
Can hide the spiderwebs, the brown.
So put the relics all back in their boxes
And with a hatchet lop the limbs
Till the trunk is naked as a cross in its bucket.

Burn them all night long in the orange roar,
The flaming sword, of long-gone Eden:
Burn them like straw in the flame that burns
At the heart of things with the unsung names
Of the one who is,

Burn the pine like frankincense:
That baby too grew up to be consumed.
You and I will sleep
On this warm hearth's holy ground
And in the morning mark our heads with ash.

THE SEAL
(for Krista Gerloff)

At first you thought it was a stone
Breaking the ripples of the outgoing tide
In the cool cove's autumn dawn.
Then looked again and saw it was a seal,
Head down like a drowned child
Drifting, lifeless, toward the shell and pebble shore.

We came down solemn from the house
And mourned as the small waves brought it close,
Mourned that a life so far from ours, and near
Should touch us only in its dying.

We waded out and touched the smooth, cool fur,
Wondering whether we should push the corpse far out
Where the ebb would take it to deep water
When the limp seal straightened, in the shallows
Opened both its eyes,
And raised a flipper in farewell, beseeching, or salute.

It was a kind of resurrection:
Any life in that heart, warm-blooded like our own
So infinitely more than none:
For the life was not yet gone
But nearly,

So we watched it ebb in joy and pain,
Waded out and fetched the seal,
Laid it on the pebbled beach:
Stroked the warm, smooth skin,
Shuddering with its breath:

And lest the beautiful, cruel gulls
Should tear it as it drifted, dying,
Hit it twice behind the head
With a staff of rotting alder wood.

I took it to the rocky point
Heavy in my arms
Like any sleeping child:
And wondered
As the deep current took it under
Shall these bones too, live?
And wondered:
How far we are from both new heaven and earth
and old.

WEDDING ON AN INCOMING TIDE

All morning long
In the cove below the house
The tide went out and out
Till algae shone green as a lawn on the rocks
And starfish clumped and drooped in the sun
As though the sea were gone for good.

On the lawn above
We set up tables for a feast
And watched the sea recede
(Beneath the grassy midden where we stood
The shells were deep as centuries)
And still the tide went out.

The mud flats stank to heaven
And stranded clams beneath the sand
Expelled their prayers in a desperate arch
That fell back to the slime.
The naked cove was littered
With broken and abandoned things.

But we readied for a wedding
Though still the tide went out:
Across a century of broken things
Begun in hope: marriages and homes and children
Stranded like fish on the drying stones
When the sea of faith withdrew.

We did not notice the change at first
But as we set up chairs on the grass

The ebbing ended. At the dry shore's edge
Each ripple cooled more of the sun-baked gravel
And as the tide of friends walked down the hill
The cove began to fill.

By the time that lunch had ended
(Under the cool, deep-rooted walnut trees)
The swells were breaking higher on the rocks
And as you stand before us on the deck
And pledge your faithfulness till death
The cool sea has returned.

Hear this, then, both of you:
However far the sea recedes, keep faith:
And He who daily fills this cove with life
Will never leave you gasping on the sand:
His blood is the life of the circling sea.
His life is yours.

THE SUNDAYS AFTER EPIPHANY
(for Mary Ruth, Heidi and Esther Ruth)

Week after week
We wake at dawn and it is still dark,
And out in Trincomali Channel
Across the invisible water
From its drowned tower under stars
Only the beacon on Walker Rock
Remembers (and remembers) the light,

Or sometimes through the open window
The cove is dark with fog, and
Even the stars are gone, and
Probing down the Channel
Only the foghorns of the freighters
(Heavy as their darkened logs)
Remind us of the world,

Which calls us even in the dark of dawn,
So we rise in the cold house:
A daughter (and her husband) and a son,
And you and I, heavy with night's increment of age,
To build a fire in the black stove;
Feed the beasts, in the graying dark, and ourselves;
And hurry down the narrow island road to church,

And over us in the car
In the deep green canyon of the road
The gray begins to glow with gold,
The alder and the cedar with silver;
Through gaps of blue the unseen sun

Carves bars across the road
Light as wind and heavy with the light,

And light through the old glass
In St. Margaret's of Galiano glistens
On the jasmine, on the willow buds:
While over the foghorn's drone we listen in the light:
"The word became flesh and dwelt among us,
And the light shines on in the dark,
And the dark could not put it out."

Outside, afterward, the sun is
Warm on our flesh, and on the road home
In the dark of our daughter's womb
The child kicks against the dark,
The touch as warm and sudden as the sun.
At home the ripples on the cove are bright,
The winter islands dark beneath a vast blue sky.

February, 1994

WOMB-WORDS

(for Father Dunstan Massey
The Abbey, Mission, B.C.)

At the abbey on the Fraser
On a sunny Monday in Lent
Below the barns, below the church
Young monks are throwing manure
Into a spreader for the pasture
On the silent, hungry hills.

And in the shed behind the barn
An old monk, a sculptor,
Throws plaster over
Fresh clay forms of angels, angels
Arched in a silent dance to welcome
A woman and the Word within her womb.

The monks work wordlessly, with care:
Young hands on the dung-smoothed wood of the forks
(Resting while the tractor makes its rounds);
Old hands bending iron to brace
A plaster womb for flowing stone
To ripen into flesh.

And I climb the green-fleshed curve
Of the fertilized hill
And wait, inside the gate of the fenced-off
Orchard of hazelnuts and pears.
In all that wide silence
There is no sound.

In the beginning was the Word:
But round the Word was the silence
Fertile as a waiting womb
Of the plaster angel-mold;
Rich as the newly-manured roots of this hill:
Wordless on an afternoon in Lent.

SOWING ON ALL SAINTS DAY

The weather is still
    and cold.

In the cove the sea is smooth as a stone.

    I have finished circling the tiny field on the small
    John Deere,
    which tears and tucks with its diesel's strength
        the corn stalks, tomato vines,
        the fallen towers of the beans,
    all that green and summer fountaining,
    back into the stony soil.

Now in the failing light
I walk its black and level length
    with a bag of winter rye, flinging
    the seed across the dirt.

Under the rising moon
    in the growing frost
    I bury the kernels

And enter the warm house
    in hope,
    only in hope:

that my ten thousand buried seeds will sprout,
that in some unimaginable summer
the field will be a multitude of new grain,
ripe, rejoicing in the wind.

FORTY YEARS
(for Erik)

You did not hear
Those first three years of life
So grew up in a wordless world
Of touch and watching (body, lips and eyes)
Till batteries and wire linked you to the rest of us.

But even then
You lived a lonely life.
New machinery in your ears
(Though shrinking as the century progressed)
Could never bridge the silence of those first three years.

Words lived in books
But not between people.
Even God was theoretical,
But things were real: the sea, the trees, the rock
And so you never took a job beneath a roof,

But planted trees,
Built houses in the rain
Crossed an ocean and discovered
Your gift of wordless listening and speech
Could lead this urban age's children nearer home.

So you are here
For wilderness and home
God is less a theory.
And we have climbed above the sea, the trees,
The glacier's great white throne, above its rounded stone.

You stand on stone
(White granite, veined with quartz)
And stretch a wrinkled nylon wad
Till light wind fills it stiff as a gull's wing,
And it lifts up, reined by the lines in your brown hands.

Writing on air
You trace the shape of peaks:
The sea, the cliff, the deep valley,
Again and again, writing with the kite
Reading the wind (*spiritus, ruach elohim*)

The gift of things,
Pouring down, pouring down,
Like torrents on the sculpted rock,
Like trickles from the snow beneath our feet
Like deep green blueberry leaves flared by frost to flame.

All is either
Gift or accident
Bubbles on vast nothingness
Or love, a gift of love poured out
To fill each thing as the wind has filled the kite,

Which is empty
Again: you fold it in
Your pack and we scramble down
And down toward the level lake and sleep:
All night on stone in the singing of waterfalls,

And then at dawn
Climb down again seaward
With the waterfall, in trees now,
Down endless stairs of cedar roots
Past fragrant rot and flourish of the forest floor.

Near noon, anticipating birthday feasts, I kneel
Beside one final waterfall, on moss
As deep as centuries, and pick
Red huckleberries: bright,
Like drops of blood.

September 13, 2007

A PROVENCE ANNUNCIATION
(for Heidi)

Chapelle
Saint-Gabriel
For seven hundred years
Has rested on its rocky hill
Beside the road from Arles to Avignon.

In March
The sun has warmed
The stones, the olive trees,
The bees within the fissured wall
(Who build their cells of honey in its dark).

The door
In front is locked.
The arch within is dark,
The space as empty as a womb.
The pilgrims and the worshippers are gone.

We watch
The sunlight bless
The pocked and sculpted stone:
The angel with her flaming sword;
The Virgin and Elizabeth, in awe.

Behind,
Two laughing girls
Look through a narrow slit
And hear their voices echo
Through the arching and abandoned vault.

They sing:
Breathe on me, breath
Of God; fill me with life. . .
Outside, in the sun, we hear the choir:
Their silver voices fill the space like the light

That poured
Its molten sword
Through the high round window
Beneath the limestone lamb of God.
And still, on the road to Arles the traffic roared.

Videos of Loren Wilkinson reading the following poems are available on Vimeo and YouTube:

"Good Friday, Up Milk Creek"
"Christmas, Whidbey Island, 1975"
"The Christ of Charlie Edenshaw"
"Gardener"
"Imago Mundi"
"Hot Cross Buns"
"The Seal"
"The Sundays after Epiphany"

Downloadable audio recordings of those poems can be found at Regent Audio, on the website for Regent College. For more information, please visit:

http://rgnt.net/imagomundi

Biographical Notes

Loren Wilkinson was two years old when his family moved to a farm in Oregon's Willamette Valley in 1943. He studied Literature and Anthropology at Wheaton College, beginning in 1961. He and Mary Ruth were married upon graduation in 1965, and he spent the next year at Johns Hopkins in their Creative Writing Seminar. From 1966 to 1969 Loren taught English at Trinity College, Chicago, while doing a Masters degree in the Philosophy of Religion at Trinity Seminary. Heidi and Erik were born in September, 1967.

They moved to Syracuse University in 1969 to do doctoral work in the Humanities, and took a teaching position at Seattle Pacific University in 1972. There the Wilkinsons began developing a groundbreaking Environmental Studies program, and in 1975 moved to Whidbey Island to live in community with the students. In 1977-78 Loren spent a year at Calvin College working with four other scholars on the book *Earthkeeping*, then three years teaching in Lincoln at the Oregon Extension of Trinity University.

Loren and Mary Ruth began teaching at Regent College in 1981, living in Vancouver until relocating in 1988 to Hunterston Farm on Galiano Island. In the decades that followed they have continued to live out a vision of mentoring, community, and care for the land that was shaped at Whidbey Island and Lincoln, Oregon. Loren is presently at work on a book, *Circles and the Cross.*

Notes on the Poems: Time and Place

Loren Wilkinson is a poet with an acute sense of place and a keen sense of occasion. As much as his poetry concerns eternal matters, each poem is firmly rooted in the particularities of time and place. They come out of his lived experience, contemplating the significance of common occurences or life events. A scientist and a Christian philosopher, his life's work involves putting together the stories of science and the stories of faith, connecting the biblical account of creation and history with the evolutionary theories of the creation and unfolding of the universe. A farmer and an artist, he pays close attention to the ebb and flow of seasons and the unfolding of the Church Year. Many poems consider Easter or Christmas, others regard the turning of tides or the way a plant grows on a rocky mountainside.

The first four pieces in this volume are from the Wilkinsons' years studying at Trinity College and Syracuse

University. "Eden's Leaves" (1968) was scrawled in a notebook during a tedious theology class, an improvisation on the professor's phrase, "Eve deceived." "Easter Maples" and "The Necessity Of Snowshoes" recall experiences of the woods in upstate New York in winter, though composition dates are uncertain, and "Easter Eggs" was written at Syracuse when Heidi and Erik were a few years old.

In 1972 Loren and Mary Ruth began teaching at Seattle Pacific University. Maps of the North Cascades were pinned to Loren's study wall. "That Tree Again" seems the perfect expression of a philosophy teacher contemplating the deep Washington woods. A Sunday hike to Mount Index took them past the Honeymoon Mine, where a metal bedstead stood abandoned in a ruined cabin. The trip inspired a potent, sexual poem that Loren considers an eco-feminist poem from before there was a label for it. Another weekend backpacking trip (probably 1973), "the kids' first trip carrying their own packs," yielded "Good Friday, Up Milk Creek." "It was like a dream" to return to the West Coast, though Loren's family had rarely visited the ocean during his Oregon childhood; "Three Ways of Facing a Storm" was inspired by Loren's first experience of canoeing on the ocean off the coast of Whidbey Island, before the Wilkinsons moved there to live and teach full time.

"Witching" is the first of five pieces written around this time, a tremendously cohesive set of poems which I consider to be among Loren's great achievements. They concern his father, his grandfather, and his childhood farming in central Oregon's Willamette Valley along the

Santiam River. Water saturates these poems; witching for springs hidden deep underground, a river baptism, rain that rots tree stumps and drips on shakes, the swollen river flooding the fields. His father died in September 1974; in "The Bloom of Carcinoma in His Bones" Loren stands beside the ocean, connected to his father by the river that runs from the family farm into the sea.

The next three poems grow out of the physical environment where the Wilkinsons spent their next two years. "Christmas, Whidbey Island, 1975" was a gift to the first group of students who lived and studied with them in SPU's Fort Casey environmental studies program; the poem culminates with an idea central to all of Wilkinson's thought: "Since God was flesh at Bethlehem, / In all the world's flesh may God be found."

"Beach Dream" comes out of a visit to Ozette, an archaeological site in Olympic National Park dubbed "the Northwest Pompei," where a huge mudslide had buried several Makah villages three centuries before. In the poem, images of the present ("nylon-sheltered walkers") overlay those of the past ("long canoes shell-adzed from straight-grained cedar") like earth that must be excavated to find the mysteries beneath. This evocation of the time of "the old ones" resonates with one of Wilkinson's most remarkable poems, written around 1976, "The Christ of Charlie Edenshaw."

In the spring of 1975, Mary Ruth visited Vancouver and became fascinated with a print at the Vancouver Museum gift shop, Roy Henry Vickers' "Christ Crucified." A year later she and Loren returned to buy the print and were introduced to Vickers himself, a Tsimshian artist who was also a Christian, who was convinced that the early response of many of the coastal First Nations people to the gospel was curiosity and a strange familiarity, "Yes, we thought so. Tell us more." That conversation built on a deep interest in the work of West Coast artists such as Charlie Edenshaw and Bill Reid, particularly Reid's sculpture at the Museum of Anthropology, "The Raven and the First Men." It led to one of the most remarkable poems in this collection.

The Wilkinsons left Seattle Pacific in 1977 for a one-year residency at Calvin College, driving across America to Grand Rapids, Michigan, with Mary Ruth's parents. An incident in Yellowstone National Park is captured in the vivid snapshot "For the Woman Who Died in the Lounge at Old Faithful Inn."

At Calvin, Loren worked on the seminal book *Earthkeeping*, as well as "Gardener," which provides the key to much of his environmental theology. The poem was written in ten minutes with hardly a word changed since, prompted by a passage in G. K. Chesterton's *The Everlasting Man* that finds significance in the women in the garden who "mistake" the risen Christ for a gardener. In the poem Wilkinson expands on the idea of Christ as the "new Adam," tending the new garden of the renewed creation, and draws a profound parallel between the earth and our human flesh, with the idea that both our bodies and our planet are in some sense also the body of Christ, physical expressions of God himself. This conviction pervades many of these poems, including "Old Faithful," "Carnelian," and "Honeymoon Mine." Also packed into this three-stanza poem is the C. S. Lewis idea that ancient myths—Greek or Roman or (as in "The Christ Of Charlie Edenshaw") West Coast Aboriginal—prefigure and prepare the way for the "true myth" of Christ.

The year at Calvin was followed by three at the Oregon Extension in Lincoln (1978-1981), half an hour from the Oregon Shakespeare Festival at Ashland, where Loren later taught several Regent summer school courses. That period is represented here by "The Green Springs," a farewell poem written at Easter, 1981, as the Wilkinsons "turn cityward to leave," headed for Vancouver and Regent College.

There are nine Vancouver poems spanning the years 1981 to 1988, with two Cambridge poems interspersed from a sabbatical in early 1986. Loren brought "Incarnicide" to a writers group he formed during his first term at Regent. It was his attempt to come to terms with a murder which had occurred within the student body just prior to his arrival. The poem expresses the writer's unease with the city, a theme he explores at greater length in "Communion in Vancouver" (Lent, 1985), an apocalyptic piece that is one of his most varied and surprising. It speaks of "this rain-washed pleasure-dome of a city":

O Vancouver, Vancouver,
(West End, Kerrisdale, Shaughnessy)
Not one stone will be left upon another...

"Wedding in October" (1983) celebrates the marriage of Dave and Sherri Koster, who will become the other full-time residents at Hunterston Farm five years later.

The poem describes a visit with writer Mike Mason en route to the Alberta wedding, and a star-lit visit to the river to watch the spawning salmon: "We watched them fling their weight across the stones, To keep a pledge made in their flesh..." During his years in Vancouver Loren wrote often for the theatre, and there are traces of this poem in his contribution to a play called *The Lonely Birch* (1987, co-authored with Tim Anderson and Ron Reed), which ends with a the fertile, hopeful image of salmon swimming upstream to breed and the U2 song, "One Tree Hill": "O great ocean, O great sea, We run like a river to the sea."

Given the demands of his Regent College teaching, Loren had to wake at an absurdly early hour to carve out time for creative writing, and sometimes found himself drifting between wakefulness and sleep. This informs several of his works in the Vancouver years. *The Lonely Birch* ends with a dreamlike, almost nightmarish image which was the remnant of a dream. With a growing sense of futility a family has waited in a Vancouver train station for their mother to join them, to travel back to their family home in Alberta. The train is about to leave when the troubled, alcoholic mother arrives, carrying in her arms an uprooted birch tree, scattering dirt on the station floor. The off-kilter, alarming climax plays on imagery established in the previous acts, ultimately bringing a fragile but powerful hope.

"Cello Concerto" (1985?) and "Nightpaths" (1987?) also explore that liminal space between waking and sleeping. The first of the Cambridge poems, "Imago Mundi" (1986) opens on just such a note ("Cast from sleep on the edge of a March dawn...") and goes on to echo the surreal imagery of "Nightpaths":

> The animals watch from the garden's verge,
> Shaped like visions of myself in the forests of my sleep,
> Though I wake to kill them and eat...

But that is only the departure point. The poem is a survey of the themes and ideas which pervade not only Wilkinson's poetry but also the whole of his writing and teaching. He considers it his most important poem. We will return to it below.

There are further connections between the world of the theatre and Loren's poetry. The last of the Vancouver poems, "Burning the Christmas Tree" (February 1988), mentions "Judy's sheep." Judy Buchan Robinson, an actress with Pacific Theatre, lived with the Wilkinsons during their time in Vancouver. She appeared in both *The Lonely Birch* and *Dreams of Kings & Carpenters*, another Christmas show to which Loren contributed, in which she played Elizabeth, spinning wool: hence the wooly tree decorations that were Judy's Christmas gifts to the company. In a Wilkinson monologue in that same play, an aged Simeon describes the dawn wind, saying, "It smelled like grass and old sheep." This is an echo of "Witching," where Loren's grandfather "smelled like oil and old sheep," suggesting that the poet finds connections between the two men, however unconsciously.

"Burning the Christmas Tree" influenced another Pacific Theatre piece, my own post-apocalyptic play, *Rem-*

nant. One of the characters imagines a lost Christ-Mass tradition of "the Old Ones," taking the branches of a Christmas tree and binding them to its stripped trunk to form the shape of the cross:

> And whenever the cold of Med Wetr would come,
> the time for the membrance of Jesus and all his doings,
> went they to the Cross Mass tree farms and laid they
>   out full many monies
> and with many prayings did choose one Cross Mass
>   tree
> for the decking of their places.

Pacific Theatre Christmas shows in those days always celebrated the Nativity "under the shadow of the cross," a theme evident in "Burning The Christmas Tree" and other of his Christmas writings. ("A girl, cruciform with pain / Grips manger boards in childbirth" ["Christmas, Whidbey Island, 1975"].)

"Imago Mundi" was written, one stanza a day, in the week leading up to Easter 1986. It was the culmination of several sabbatical months spent in Cambridge developing an early version of his book, *Circles and the Cross*. A dense poem, it sets itself the ambitious task of mapping the seven days of Creation onto the seven days of Holy Week—Eden and Easter, the two biblical events which he explores in so much of his writing—and touches on many of the themes that inform the rest of his work. Exactly a year later comes "Hot Cross Buns" (1987), a more approachable piece that remembers Good Friday in Cambridge the year before.

In 1988 the Wilkinsons moved to Hunterston Farm on Galiano Island. "The Seal" (1989?) was written soon after the move, for a Regent student from the Czech Republic. "Wedding on an Incoming Tide" was written for their daughter Heidi's wedding in the summer of 1990, a marvelously specific poem that evokes a palpable sense of the physical place, the same bay that provides the setting for "The Seal." In the movement of the tide it finds the rhythm of marriage; he looks at his daughter's marriage with the same unsentimental yet hopeful realism found in "Wedding in October" several years earlier. "The Sundays after Epiphany" (February 1994), "Womb-Words" (Spring 1995?) and "Sowing on All Saints Day" (200?) continue the project of tracing the flow of the seasons within the movements of the Church calendar, and interweave imagery of pregnancy and birth with Christmas and Easter themes of incarnation and resurrection.

Loren closes the collection with two of his tenderest poems, "Forty Years" (September 2007) and "A Provence Annunciation" (March 2014), crafted for birthdays of his two grown children.

Thanks to Karen Cooper for her careful editing of the Notes to these poems.

Ron Reed
Vancouver, BC

Notes on the Poems:
Language

"Raven's children loved the touch of things." So says my favourite of Loren's poems, "The Christ Of Charlie Edenshaw." Just so, the poet loves the sound of things; he loves what words mean, of course, but he loves them also for themselves, and for the real things they stand in for.

In *The Dyer's Hand*, W.H. Auden wrote "the sign that a beginner has a genuine original talent is that he is more interested in playing with words than in saying something original," and the first poem in this collection introduces us to a young writer intoxicated with language. The assonance of the lecturer's expression "Eve deceived" becomes the germ of a poem that's all about wordplay: he savours the long vowel sounds of "Eden's leaves," "weaves," "speech," "beasts bleed," "Eve seeks;" he plays with the dual meanings of "leaves," as both noun and verb; he twins the expressions "violet light" and "violent light." The poem is language-dense, as much a word puzzle as a poem, but with subtle musical touches that make it more than a cerebral exercise. It's no surprise that this young poet will have a life-long love of the compact intricacies and theological complexity of Gerard Manley Hopkins.

Read these poems aloud. Let the words take flesh, feel them in your mouth: the lips, the teeth, the tip of the tongue. The ease of the long vowels in the opening line collide immediately with the dense and crunchy consonants in the second. You can't read "Hide lost beasts" quickly or easily, and the reader is forced to slow down and pay attention. Then the intricacy lifts into something more lyrical and fanciful—"Lion's song, Hawk's speech"—before settling into stricter rhymes and a certain rhythmic momentum. There's a lot going in on those first eleven syllables. Read that opening stanza aloud a few times, observing the line ends with the slightest pause, and hear the musical flow of it, three three-note bars in 4/4 time, then the subtlest shift with a two-note measure.

This is a poem about language, and language is part of what was broken in the Fall. Now lions sing no longer, and hawks don't speak ("beasts are dumb"), and now they bleed—perhaps a parallel to the child-bearing pain suggested by Eve eating the "fruit of the moon." It's also a poem about identity, distorted by sin; Eve is "dis-Eved" and ends up seeking her lost face, an echo of *Till We Have Faces*, a book Loren was teaching at the time in an Inklings course.

It is fitting that this collection opens with a poem set in the garden of Eden. Creation, in both the broadest and most specific senses, is central to Loren's life and work. The Genesis account of Creation resonates throughout his poetry, and garden imagery is everywhere. Adam's priestly task of naming Creation (carried on in the work of both scientist and poet) is often suggested, and the seven days of Creation provide the structure for "Imago Mundi," which Loren considers "the most important poem I've written."

The other recurring Biblical story is that of Christ's Passion. Death and resurrection are constant themes, and no fewer than nine of these thirty-five poems were written specifically for Lent or Easter. The seven stanzas of "Imago Mundi" were written one per day through Holy Week, mapping the events of Christ's passion onto the template of Creation.

Add the idea and pervasive imagery of incarnation—the embodiment of the eternal God in the man Jesus, the sacramental presence of spiritual realities in nature and in human nature, the way the earth is like a human body and human bodies are like the earth and both are dwelling-places for God—and you have Loren's three great themes; creation, incarnation, and resurrection.

It's fascinating to read the second poem selected for this volume and find the writer using a similar musical strategy to open a very different poem. With terrific economy, a succession of delicious long "e" sounds and their strong, easy rhythm—"geometries of maple trees / freeze in the sleet"—are abruptly arrested not only by the full stop after "sleet," but by another consonant cluster as dense as the second line of "Eden's Leaves." Attention must be paid, as we sound out the phrase "But the roots slant down" before releasing into the lyricism of "Between the limestone and the frost / And know..." Still, this poem is less dense and idea-heavy than its predecessor, a tangible and specific observation of a tree in a winter forest that puts one in mind of the work of another poet of the American East Coast, Robert Frost. The theology is there, the resonance with the events of the first Easter, but the tree and the forest come first: the meaning, the metaphor emerge from them as naturally as syrup from a maple tree, so long as there is a poet to drive in the spike, and notice. "If a tree falls in a forest..."

Plants are everywhere in this lush little grove of poems. The 97 sparse syllables of that first poem give us leaves, fruit, steep trees, thistles, dry weeds. The maple tree and the one on Calvary are the whole focus of "Easter Maples," and the rest of the collection is dense with "living wood;" alder, ash, pine, hazel, cottonwood, thrusting grass by a choked pear-tree, wheat, weeds, fir stumps, cottonwoods, plum trees, boysenberries, bleeding-heart, deep green blueberry leaves, wild violets in the grass, skunk cabbage, ferns, salal, trilliums, camas, watercress, bulbs and roots and rhizomes, the rot of leaves, jasmine, willow buds, thickets, the twigs and tendrils of a wood, Birnam wood, "Beauty's briar," a lonely birch, a Christmas tree that hints of green wilderness, lichens, moss as deep as centuries, red huckleberries "bright, like drops of blood," algae "green as a lawn," manzanita twigs, corn stalks, tomato vines, the fallen towers of the beans, winter rye, new grain, orchard of hazelnuts and pears, deep-rooted olive trees, "spruce-root, twisted into cord." Sleep-crowding woods, tree-splitting roots, a water-witching stick whose "lopped-off roots have left their longings in the wood." His father's hands are like kindling, carcinoma is a plant that blooms, a lung is a dark-branched shrub. Old women and men are like trees walking.

But most of all, the cedar: dripping cedar woods, cedar burl that's whorled like nebulae, sea-shaped cedar, heron-sheltering cedar, cedar scent, mortised cedar built into a house, capes of shredded cedar stripped in spring from trees by forest-walkers, storm-stopping cedar split into planks, cedar shavings, canoes shell-adzed from straight-grained cedar, the living cedar wood that contains the full-fleshed forms "of eagle, whale, mosquito, bear, beaver, deer and man."

I think of *The Shoddy Lands*, a C.S. Lewis story in which an Oxford professor has a vision of the world through another's eyes:

Everything seemed curiously blurred... There were upright shapes, vaguely green in colour, but of a very dingy green. I peered at them for quite a long time before it occurred to me that they might be trees. I went nearer and examined them; and the impression they made on me is not ieasy to put in to words. 'Trees of a sort,' or, 'Well, trees, if you call *that* a tree,' or, 'And attempt at trees,' would come near it. They were the crudest shabbiest apology for trees you could imagine. They had no real anatomy, no real branches even; they were more like lamp-posts with great, shapeless blobs of green stuck on top of them. Most children could draw better trees from memory.

Loren's world is not shoddy. He knows his trees; he has examined them, they have anatomy and scent and texture and cycles of life, and he can put it all into words.

Constantin Stanislavski called generality "the enemy of art." It is also the enemy of science, and of life in Christ: "Therefore, if any man be in Christ, he is a new creation: old things are passed away; behold, all things are become new."

An artist, a scientist, and a priest descended from Adam, Loren can name each creature—vegetable, animal, or mineral—and offers up each stone as an act of oblation: icy stone, dusty stones, coloured stones, lucid stones, sun-baked gravel, bleaching rocks, gold-flecked quartz, the green sheen of malachite, diorite, galena, granite, limestone, fool's gold, molten silver, melted glass, iron, agate, argilite, andesite, carnelian, fresh clay, sculpted rock, river-rolled basalt, flood-dug rubble, boulders, geysers, mudpots, fumaroles, sulpher, silt, muck, mud and lava dust, brown bluffs, a well dug down to bedrock, rich rock breaking beneath a pick, silt flats, sand, a tide-scooped gravel spit, a shell and pebble shore.

In *An Offering Of Uncles: The Priesthood of Adam and the Shape of the World*, a book Loren frequently teaches, Robert Farrar Capon describes family trips to the rocky beaches of Long Island, picking out particular stones for their beauty or their usefulness:

> We walk down the beach lifting stones into our history: we are collectors, ingatherers of being. Man is the lover of textures, colors and shapes—the only

creature in the whole world who knows a good pickling stone when he sees one. The arts go way beyond that; but that is where they begin.... As long as man can hunt stones, he will know that the fire of his priesthood has not gone out.

Loren's poems are such an oblation, an offering up of what the poet sees. And like the priest who lifts up the common elements of bread and wine to become (or be revealed as?) the body and blood of Christ, the poet's act of paying attention, giving thanks and offering up has the power to renew those of us who take and eat.

To return to the poems themselves, I can't help overlaying "Easter Eggs" with that passage from Capon, which I've heard Loren read often enough that my mind's ear hears it in his voice. The poet's children hunt eggs, the priest's kids discover stones, and the women in the garden find "an unexpected spring." This is one of Loren's less dense and complex poems, and I love it for its lightness and apparent childlike simplicity. The form fits the function, especially in that second stanza, which has the rhythm, shape, and imagery of a nursery rhyme. I think the room that "hides sweetness like a tree" suggests an apple tree (Eden's tree?), its colourful red fruit hidden among verdant leaves, a hidden sweetness echoes that of his previous Easter poem, where the "pierced trees / pump their sweetness into pails."

The poem was prompted by a passage in Chapter Five of *Reflections on the Psalms* by C. S. Lewis:

There is a stage in a child's life at which it cannot separate the religious from the merely festal character of Christmas or Easter. I have been told of a very small and very devout boy who was heard murmuring to himself on Easter morning a poem of his own composition which began "Chocolate eggs and Jesus risen." This seems to me, for his age, both admirable poetry and admirable piety. But of course the time will soon come when such a child can no longer effortlessly and spontaneously enjoy that unity. He will become able to distinguish the spiritual from the ritual and festal aspect of Easter; chocolate eggs will no longer be sacramental. And once he has distinguished he must put one or the other first.

The last of the Syracuse poems was probably written at Seattle Pacific, remembering back. "The Necessity of Snowshoes" is one of Loren's best, paying tribute to New England's poet laureate Robert Frost and his beloved "Stopping by Woods on a Snowy Evening" and "The Road Not Taken." As these woods fill up with snow, we leave roads altogether and strike out deeper into the woods themselves, held up by snowshoes. The solid, practical instructions of the third stanza are given by a man who knows exactly how to fashion snowshoes from an ash tree (Loren can show you a hand-crafted snowshoe from Syracuse days), but the specificity of the image opens into the poem's gloriously apt metaphor. There are hints early on—the invocation of Frost, the possibility that our pointedness might suggest a pen—but only once the forest and the workshop are tangible to us does he reveal that what's on his mind is the power of literature. The rawhide is "slippery as worms, or words" because poems themselves are the things that hold us up, give us paths through "the world's white wilderness," leading us to visions we would never have if we stuck to the roads ("snow-cliffs that the stream cuts deep"). The poem concludes with the reassuring resolution of that final rhyme, "deep" and "sleep." Back to Robert Frost, and the conclusion of his snowy evening: " . . . promises to keep / and miles to go before I sleep."

"Snowshoes" introduces a cluster of poems about leaving behind roads and cities to strike out into the wilderness. The philosopher-poet's next piece pays tribute to a philosopher rather than a poet, and we find the famous falling tree "in the secret place / at the center of all woods" where wood ducks are "bright as clowns," an unspoiled place that suggests Eden before the fall, a hidden glade not yet spoiled by man. "Good Friday, Up Milk Creek" is the reflection of the scientist-poet on a weekend family trek into the North Cascades which Loren remembers vividly; "There was a spring sale at R.E.I. We bought the kids their own back packs. It was their first trip carrying their own." The winter has left skunk cabbage leaves pressed flat and palm-shaped, "white as children's hands." Heidi and Erik were about six. "Facing a Storm" was inspired by canoe trips on the open ocean, prefiguring the Regent College boat course Loren and Mary Ruth led for so many summers out of Galiano Island. Again, the poem subtly invokes Easter as it considers three responses to a storm at sea: the Maundy Thursday jellyfish, whose body and blood are the ocean itself; Jonah's Good Friday entombment; and Jesus' otherworldly Easter Sunday peace in the face of fear, His calm mastery of the seas, and death itself.

This is another poem that must be read aloud, for the pleasure of the steady iambic pulse of the language, the tactility of "crystalline collapse," the matter-of-fact economy of "The quiet sailors / Tidy up their ship / In terror of his God," the heightened verbal richness and breathtaking imagery of the final stanza ("His sea-salt blood, his mammal's flesh) / With fishscales in his hair"), the sudden assonance of "Wind's waves will not wake him" and the proclamation "Peace, sea, he speaks." Loren loves that long "e" sound, and uses it to shift the poem to the still beauty of its final lines.

"The Honeymoon Mine" is one of Loren's finest and most significant poems, along with "The Necessity of Snowshoes," "The Christ Of Charlie Edenshaw," "Imago Mundi," "The Seal," "Wedding on an Incoming Tide," the set of five poems about Loren's childhood and father, and—probably to Loren's surprise—two particular favourites of my own, "For the Woman Who Died in the Lounge at Old Faithful Inn" and perhaps "Communion in Vancouver." "The Honeymoon Mine" is a deftly-drawn character study, a dark story told with power and economy. In terms of imagery, this is an extraordinarily cohesive poem, continually identifying the miner with the hard stone of the mountain, and setting him at odds with fertile, growing things and the rain that gives them life. From the very outset he is, "A rootless man with treasure in his head," tripping on roots and cursing "the rock-obscuring bounty of the rain."

The sexuality of the poem is arresting. "He wanted hidden things laid bare," and "stripped the dirt away from stone." He drives a tunnel deep into the mountain, but the sound of dripping water:

> ...haunted his dark with images of life:
> Cedar-smell, and ferns like girls' hair;
> Salal leaves smooth as flesh,
> And blueberries crushed into juice
> On his rockdust-covered tongue.

There is a remarkable shift in diction in the third section. After the rich and complex imagery that precedes it, the language is suddenly stripped to an alarming, business-like plainness:

> He built a cabin:
> Roofed with cedar,
> Bolted to the rock,
> He waited out the pressure of the snow
> And in the spring
> He went to town and got a wife.

The "honeymoon" consummation that follows is abrupt, elemental, disturbing. The vein plays out, the girl leaves, "Scared out by his stony hands, his anger at the rock." As Loren has said, the piece is an expression of eco-feminism before he had encountered the term.

The poem has other intricacies. The mine is found along the trail to Mount Index, which stands out from the landscape around it like a stone finger. The man "dug beneath the waterfall, / Poking one long empty thumb / Into the mountain's side," an image that suggests not only a sort of sexual violation, but also Saint Thomas, who also "wanted hidden things laid bare," mysteries made clear.

I wonder if a young man's thoughts inevitably turn back to his own childhood around the time he turns thirty, when he is finally, undeniably, grown up. Perhaps young fathers begin to contemplate their fathers as they begin to raise their own children. Being immersed in the lives of children stirs memories of one's own childhood. In Loren's case, his return to the Pacific Northwest and proximity to his aging father prompted a suite of five glorious, deeply-felt poems about fathers and sons, rivers and oceans, about childhood and coming of age and, finally, dying.

It is a privilege to see the poet's work as a whole, to see the connections between the poems, to map them onto the seasons and settings of his life. These five works were not intended as a set; they're simply expressions of what happened to be on his mind for a while. They don't intentionally pick up the themes and techniques of the works that preceded them; they just grow from the same soil, build on foundations that have already been laid.

"Witching," which concerns the mysterious but commonplace folk-art of water-witching, rather than anything to do with witchcraft, takes up elements of a poem very unlike it, "The Honeymoon Mine." The poem is sexual, if awkwardly so: it is, after all, a snapshot of a young boy embarassed by his grandfather's zeal, his closeness, and perhaps the erectness of the "wise white root." And where the stone-hearted, treasure-headed miner's tunneling "to the peak's stone core" is cold and fruitless ("The vein played out by summer's end. / The girl left by Christmas"), Grandpa's "own root delved daddy and myself / From the well of grandma's womb." There is a robust, healthy masculinity here that stands in contrast to the miner's, and stone's enmity toward plants and water is here reconciled in the poem's final stanza. Grandpa's stone hands end up in the dirt. Fertile, though, he flourishes underground, his hands transubstantiated into witching wands, "like hazels sending roots in search of rain."

"Baptism" recreates with exquisite precision a scene from Loren's youth that stands in for the whole world of distinctly American Christianity he grew up in. It is like something out of Flannery O'Connor or Robert Duval's film *The Apostle*, but without their darkness. The tractor abandoned at the end of a Saturday in the fields, because of course the men wouldn't be working on Sunday, "Disc-deep in clods / And cold as a troll." What a delicious phrase! Just for the language of it, and also for its understated reference to Tolkien's trolls who turned to stone when caught by the sun. The potluck dinner of jello and baked beans takes on Old Testament significance: "Come to the waters, every one that thirsts, and he that hath no money; buy, and eat, without money and without price." The water itself, as ominous and threatening as in the poem "In Winter's Wet in Oregon," is hard and unyielding. The boy is "scared to death of it," and it takes force to enter: force of will, and the preacher's shove. But, Easter-like, he rises up and finds himself rooted deep, and "green with the water's life."

The poem contains an arresting phrase which recurs in a much later poem, "Forty Years (for Erik)." "The great white throne of glaciers" is drawn from George MacDonald's *Unspoken Sermons*, excerpted in C. S. Lewis's *George MacDonald: An Anthology*:

Is oxygen-and-hydrogen the divine idea of water? God put the two together only that man might separate and find them out? He allows His child to pull his toys to pieces: but were they made that he might pull them to pieces? ... There is no water in oxygen, no water in hydrogen; it comes bubbling fresh from the imagination of the living God, rushing from under the great white throne of the glacier. The very thought of it makes one gasp with an elemental joy no metaphysician can analyze.

Loren's grief at his father's death finds expression in "The Bloom of Carcinoma in His Bones." He chooses a rigorously metrical sonnet form, as though such primal emotion needs established form to contain it and allow it to be spoken. As Emily Dickinson writes, "After great pain, a formal feeling comes." The poem must be read aloud, its measured five-beat lines allowed to move in quiet procession. Hear the carefully structured rhymes—bones, burned, turned, stones; flow, hills, bills, slow. Sense the slight disruptions in the rhythm as the break approaches, then the return to perfect scansion for that middle line, standing alone, the transition point from river to sea: "The ocean drew its river like a tide."

If the iambic pentameter suggests Shakespeare, the off-rhythm "Out and out" must surely echo Macbeth, "Out, out, brief candle!" Then the final stanza falls back into rhythm, pairs of weak and strong syllables walking in step toward the unexpected, out-of-rhythm release of that final line; "Like some great beast running, running toward the sun."

The conflation of human bodies and the "body" of the earth—stone hands and womb-wells, mountains like fingers, hands like kindling, cancer blooming in bones—runs through these poems, and culminates in "Carnelian." The river itself is alive, has a body—an elbow, rainy fingers—and the young Loren is acutely aware of his own body, and his father's, when they strip and step into its cold flow. His father points out the stone that's just as alive, "An agate, bigger than his fists, / Banded, pink and clear like flesh, / fresh-cut, too pained to bleed." That stone ends up an image of his father's heart: fascinating that in "Honeymoon Mine" the comparison of flesh and stone made the man seem harder, where here it makes the stone softer. I love the diction of his father's phrase, "That there's carnelian," and the boy's recognition that the City of God is formed from the flesh-coloured, heart-sized rock. "Carne" means flesh, and that awareness echoes through words the poet uses repeatedly: incarnation, carnelian, incarnicide. The cumulative effect of this pervasive imagery gives one the sense that everything in creation—human bodies and souls, the earth and its foliage and all its creatures—not only bears the image and likeness of its Creator, but that God is in some very real sense embodied in it all, as He was in Jesus. Certainly there is something unique in God's incarnation in Christ, but it must also be true that our "family resemblance" to our Father, and the resonances of that in everything He created, must run deep.

"Christmas, Whidbey Island, 1975" is the manifesto of that idea, concluding, "Since God was flesh at Bethlehem / In all the world's flesh may God be found." The opening stanza builds a beautifully observed panorama of the natural world as its rhetoric builds a growing curiosity through a series of negations; not, not, nor, nor, neither, nor, in nothing. What is it that's not in the waves or the heron or seashells or the galaxy? The final lines give the apparent and, in a Wilkinson poem, unexpected, answer, "In nothing of his bright, shy world" (gorgeous phrase) "May God the fathering be found." A stanza break makes us hold on to that uncharacteristic denial for a moment before the reversal of the next line, "If not found first in Bethlehem." A ringing affirmation, made more potent by the series of negations and reversals that come before. God's son and God's creation have flesh, and bear the image and likeness of their Father: *Imago Dei*, *Imago Mundi*. Indeed, he is the "thousand-fleshed god," according to "The Christ of Charlie Edenshaw."

At the heart of this, one of Wilkinson's most accomplished poems, is the idea that throughout literature, throughout history, in cultures all over the world, God has inspired versions of the Christ story, and when people encounter the actual story of Jesus, the way will have been prepared. Rene Girard explores the idea at length. It was J. R. R. Tolkien's argument in a midnight conversation on Addison's Walk that led C. S. Lewis to embrace the "true myth" of Christ, after a lifelong fascination with stories about dying and reviving gods. In a conversation with Loren and Mary Ruth, Tsimshian artist Roy Henry Vickers described his people's historic responsiveness to the Christian gospel in just this way, finding resonances between the Biblical narrative and many First Nations stories and traditions, particularly those of the trickster/creator Raven.

The poem begins with something of an invocation, suggesting both First Nations ritual and Christian liturgy. The three carefully fashioned stanzas, each introducing one of the sections which follow, suggest that Raven is himself a trinity. The first section uses a rhetorical pattern not unlike that of the preceding poem, setting up a rising tension with its unresolved repetition ("they knew," "they knew," "they knew") before its resolution in the final two lines. The poet revels in the sound of these tribal names, and with their invocation creates a sense of ceremony and mystery, and the growing awareness of a vast and varied multitude of people who knew... what? "That Raven, Raven is the bringer of the light." It smacks of oral tradition; it is the technique of a storyteller, capturing the attention of his listeners with repetition and growing suspense. Again, as always, read this poem aloud.

Just as "Raven's children loved the touch of things," and loved finding the shapes of creatures in the cedar, so the poet loves the shapes of words, their feel in the mouth:

Opalescent abalone,
Winking from a bear's carved head;
Argilite, like ebony.
Goat's wool,
Seal-skin,
Spruce-root, twisted into cord:
The glory of the thing—

Glorious indeed. The poet is like the carver, and the carver is like God himself, "Whose own hands carved the earth."

Finally, in the story of Raven escaping from the smoke-hole trap to bring the sun, moon, stars, fresh water and fire to the world, Loren finds a figure of resurrection, and links the image of the cedar, which has taken on such potency through the course of the poem, to the wood of the cross. This is a masterful poem; the use of language is vivid and subtle, the sense of time and place potent, the ideas complex, the interweaving of eras and mythologies and metaphors intricate and compelling.

"Beach Dream" continues the poet's contemplation of "the old ones," of the civilization that thrived on the "rain-blest coast" of the Pacific Northwest millenia ago. It is fascinating to find the many ways this poem and "Charlie Edenshaw" are inter-related. Here Wilkinson experiments with a complex poetic form, the sestina; each of the six six-line stanzas uses the same words for line endings, in an intricate rotating pattern, then repeats those six words in a final three-line "envoi." Particularly interesting is his play with the word "walkers" and various hyphenated modifiers, which refer to ancient First Nations people ("for-est-walkers"), modern hikers ("nylon-sheltered walkers," "rain-proof land-bound walkers"), herons ("ever-watching walkers"), or all ("years and tears of rain-soaked walkers"), a layering of times and creatures that is the essence of the poem.

I love Loren's 1977 piece "For the Woman Who Died in the Lounge at Old Faithful Inn." Loren was surprised when I told him so; I think he favours the more complex, substantial poems, packed dense with ideas. But I love the clarity and simplicity of this snapshot of a poem, and its compassion. On a long road trip, driving the family's possessions from Washington to Michigan, the Wilkinsons stopped overnight in Yellowstone Park. From the balcony of their room they saw a woman die of a heart attack, and this poem grew out of Loren imagining who that woman might have been. It pictures a woman very unlike him, a tourist unfamiliar with even this National Park version of wilderness (a great elk grazes beside a traffic jam, the sky seen through the lens of an instant camera), and her perhaps more mundane, or at least naïve, version of awe at what she sees. She may not truly grasp what she is seeing in a geyser, and perhaps her mind should not wander to a thing so ordinary as her grandchildren—or is there something holy in that impulse, the wish to share the experience with children she loves? The poet knows the particulars of the geological phenomena—geysers, mudpots, fumaroles, andesite—but the woman is mostly struck by how hot they are, and her comment comes off like a commonplace about the weather. Still, wonder is wonder, and I find myself moved by the innocence of her reactions.

In the fourth stanza, something more ominous begins to bubble up through the poem. The poet finds a connection between the pools of Yellowstone Park and the pool of Bethesda in Chapter 5 of John's gospel, where the sick waited for the stirring of the waters to be healed. The woman "saw the troubled waters bulge / but did not move," and by evening she was dead. And here the poem picks up the thread that has run through so many of the poems: "You felt, through andesites of pain, / The geysers of your blood go up." As foreign as the woman is to this more primal world, her body and the body of the earth are... Alike? The same? One? At the very least, they are part of the same Creation, fashioned in the image of the same Creator.

"Gardener" was written the following spring working on the book *Earthkeeping*, and Wilkinson's focused thought on these questions over the course of many months results in a poem where these themes emerge with acute clarity. It shows us Mary Magdalene on Easter morning, in the garden where Jesus' tomb was:

> The flowers in the rock
> The grass
> The gnarled, deep rooted olive trees
> Were rooted in his flesh

Christ is himself a garden, from which the world grows. But he also plays another role:

She thought he was the gardener
Then saw He was the Christ
But still she was mistaken...
For Christ was gardener of that place

Loren was reading G.K. Chesterton's book *The Everlasting Man* when he came on a passage at the end of the chapter "The Strangest Story in the World":

On the third day the friends of Christ coming at daybreak to the place found the grave empty and the stone rolled away. In varying ways they realised the new wonder; but even they hardly realised that the world had died in the night. What they were looking at was the first day of a new creation, with a new heaven and a new earth; and in a semblance of the gardener God walked again in the garden, in the cool not of the evening but the dawn.

He set the book aside and wrote this poem in ten minutes, "The quickest, easiest poem I ever wrote, and I've hardly changed a word since."

Loren is correct when he sees this as a key poem. Of the many metaphors that personify the nature and work of God, we often particularly identify with those which connect with our own experience. David was a shepherd; he was inspired to see the Lord as his shepherd. I am an actor, and am particularly moved by the Philippians passage that has Christ setting aside his godly form to take on the character of a human servant. Loren is many things, but he was raised a farmer, and regardless of his academic pursuits he remains a gardener, both in the literal sense of planting and tending and harvesting the bounty of his garden at Hunterston Farm, and in the broader sense of stewarding the larger creation. There is probably no idea closer to Loren's heart than this. The earth is a garden, the flesh is a garden, and each New Adam its gardener, made in the image of Christ who, as well as being the garden's creator, is himself both garden and gardener. Years later, Loren would underscore the importance of the gardener figure in his essay "Unheroic Gardeners: The Necessary Failure in The Lord of the Rings Films," presented at a University of St. Andrew's symposium marking the 65th anniversary of Tolkien's Lang Lecture "On Fairy-stories" (1939). He draws attention to Samwise, Tom Bombadil, the ents, Faramir, and even Gandalf as gardeners, and connects them all to Christ:

> The Christian story too is about the centrality of surrendering power—indeed, about gardening. Not only does the story begin in a garden but at its climax, the hero, returning from his underground journey is rightly mistaken—as so many medieval portrayals show him—as a gardener. The unheroic gardner is the hero of Tolkien's story—and of the even greater Christian story which informs it.

"Gardener" also picks up a thread from "The Christ of Charlie Edenshaw," that Christ is very much like the gods of this world's myths, who also create, who also die and rise again, "Persephone, Osiris, Gaia, or only wild Pan."

But Christ is different in an essential way; He is also "the God beyond the world / Who made it." It is interesting that in *The Everlasting Man* Chesterton also plays with the comparison between the gods of myth and the true God in Christ; in the chapter "The God of the Cave," he distinguishes Jesus born in a cave from Mithras who "sprung alive out of a rock," or Pallas "from the brain of Zeus." It seems these themes also informed Loren's poem.

"The Green Springs" again sees earth as a living body, and finds in the natural flow of seasons and centuries, and in the unnatural human activity of logging, a cycle of crucifixion, death, and hoped-for resurrection. The occasion of the poem is the Wilkinsons leaving the Trinity Extension program and the mountains around Lincoln, Oregon to move to Regent College and the city, Vancouver. The title refers in part to the Green Springs Highway, the road they travelled on their departure which winds precipitously down from Lincoln to Ashland and the I-5. There had been an earthquake not long before, and the poem surveys a mutilated landscape: the water filled with silt, things shaken up way down deep. It is a poem both of grief and hope, the faith that even skeletons may be leafed with green.

Again, pay attention to the words. Like Annie Dillard, another poet who delights in the names of things, Wilkinson makes a litany of places and growing things: Soda Mountain, Chinquapin, Hobart's Bluff; trilliums, camas, watercress, bulbs and roots and rhizomes; Keene Creek, and the Klamath, and the sea. The last syllable of each line rhymes precisely with the first word of the next, lending the poem a propulsive momentum that emulates the steep drive down the mountain from Lincoln to the interstate below, with an ever so slight easing up as we reach the bottom of the hill and the poem's conclusion.

"Incarnicide" was the first poem Loren wrote after arriving at Regent College. He brought it to a writers' group he started up among the students for which I owe a life-long debt of gratitude; invited into the group, I had never thought of myself as a writer before, but it was the first of a series of such groups I've been part of, right to the present day. The poem was an attempt to give some sort of expression to the grief and shock which hit the close-knit Regent community following a murder within the student body. He struggled fruitlessly with it until he decided to use a complex poetic structure that would provide a shape and rigour which might harness something of the intensity and chaos of the event, as he did when writing about the death of his own father in "The Bloom of Carcinoma in his Bones." As T. S. Eliot wrote, "To use very strict form is a help, because you concentrate on the technical difficulties of mastering the form, and allow the content of the poem a more unconscious and freer release." The highly technical demands of the form allowed Wilkinson to engage with a highly disturbing story that was difficult to approach.

The form is something of a hybrid of the sestina, where specific line-endings rotate from stanza to stanza according to a strict pattern (as in "Beach Dream"), and the villanelle, where it is the rhyme scheme that shifts. It is interesting to consider Philip K. Jason's observation that the "villanelle is often used to deal with one or another degree of obsession," in poems such as "Mad Girl's Love Song" by Sylvia Plath. Its convoluted and constrained structure of repetition can create "a feeling of dislocation and a paradigm for schizophrenia." Intentional or not, the form is well-suited to this examination of a disordered mind and soul.

The poem is a fiction, a dark variation on the Eden story from the perspective of another Adam, who moves from being alone, naming creation in the shadow of his namer, to union with a woman, "flesh with my flesh," to something like the Cain and Abel story. The language here is dense, difficult, and at times obscure, twisted and tormented like the soul at the heart of its story. Loren has never been satisfied with the poem. It is included here for the ambition of what it sets out to accomplish, and for extraordinary passages which are among the most powerful in any Wilkinson poem:

> . . . I pierced you to your sick heart's core
> And dragged your bleeding body to this river by the
>   sea
> And scooped a grave from silt beneath this alder tree,
> Shoveled muck back over your eyes, your thighs, your
>   hair,
> Which will twist my life no longer: you will name my
>   world no more.

While the actual murder and concealment of the body occurred outside the Vancouver area, Loren re-imagines the events on a stretch of beach where he often went running, below the Museum of Anthropology, in the shadow of an eerie, looming stand of enormous alder trees. "Wreck Beach" is another poem set in the same place, during the same period, with which this forms something of a diptych, and with which the poet is equally dissatisfied. But it is intriguing to see the mythic imagery of Eden and the Fall play through both poems. The first focuses on Adam, alone, and the enmity that then arose between the man and the woman; the second contemplates nakedness and shame, the innocence and fallenness of sexuality. Both are set in this patch of something like wilderness found in the shadow of the city, and reflect the poet's unease with urban life. This ambivalence is expressed in this scrap of an unfinished poem not included here:

> Not yet Zion or Gomorrah
> The towers of this city stand
> Between the mountains and the sand:
>
> If not today, perhaps tomorrow
> We will satisfy each sense
> And recover innocence...

The same themes emerge in "Communion in Vancouver," and that same beach gets an understated name check. God rains on "this rain-washed pleasure-dome of a city," while the same rain falls on "the wrack and wreck of a winter beach." The poem is another of my own favourites, observational and sharply drawn as a portfolio of street photography. This is particularly true of the splendid second section, reminiscent of the Polaroid snapshot of a poem Loren captured at the Old Faithful Inn. "Communion" is less densely wrought than the poems that precede it, seemingly more loose-limbed and improvisatory, a sketchbook of impressions, characters and events grouped around phrases from the Anglican Communion liturgy. Perhaps another metaphor is closer to the reality of the poem; the highly varied and contrasting pieces of the poem are like the separate pieces of coloured glass in a church window, which taken together create a vivid image. Indeed, the stained glass windows of St. John's Shaughnessy are central to the work; they include shards from the original windows of Canterbury Cathedral, recovered after its bombing in 1942. The poem was written around the time Loren played the Prior of Christchurch in a Pacific Theatre production of Dorothy Sayers' *The Zeal Of Thy House*, the story of architect William of Sens building Canterbury Cathedral in the 12ᵗʰ century.

Though set in a peaceful parish church on a rainy Sunday morning, this is a poem about war and crucifixion. The silver-haired woman who slips "in the cross of the road" bears the image of Christ as she is helped up by two friends, "one on her right and one on her left." On its surface, the third section would seem to be mostly about rain, but even here war is subtly evoked with a reference to Edith Sitwell's deeply Christian war poem "Still Falls The Rain (The Raids, 1940, Night and Dawn)," which ends with a portrait of Christ's sacrifice, "Still do I love, still shed my innocent light, my Blood, for thee." The fourth and fifth sections of "Communion in Vancouver" turn their attention to the stained glass windows of St. John's, "Blown eight hundred years ago / From a molten, brilliant mass / In Canterbury"; I like the play with the word "mass." These sections touch on the murder of Thomas Becket, the Battle of Britain, and the WW2-era figures in one of the windows; there is a pointed ambiguity and ambivalence about the praying soldier whose "rifle points at the earth." Is it an image of peace, the weapon at rest, not poised to kill? Or does it suggest that the earth itself is a victim of war? In the context of the poems that have gone before, it does not seem a reassuring image.

It is section six which raises the poem and its rhetoric to a higher level, an alarming vision of destruction as sudden and violent as the nuclear holocaust it describes. Opening with the cadence of Christ's mourning over the apocalypse that would beset Jerusalem, the poet pulls together the varied threads of the poem into a vision of destruction; "Perhaps" (and only perhaps) "these concrete arches still will stand" (even though they are concrete). He describes the blackened cross, the burnt dome like Hiroshima, the melting of the Canterbury glass again, but for the last time. This will truly be the war to end all wars. The horror is sharpened by the matter-of-fact details of the bombing:

> ...the Canterbury glass
> Will have shattered one last time:
> On the north from the harbor bomb
> On the south from the blasts

At the Trident base in its quiet place
On Puget Sound

These are succeeded by the heightened poetic imagery of the final stanza, pulling together all the poem's imagery and themes—blood, glass, fire, blood, rain, the people of St. John's, communion, the city—in one catastrophic vision:

And the ancient blood-red glass
Will melt again and flow like blood;
The molten silver candlesticks
Will drip like rain
Where now the people kneel, at communion
In Vancouver.

Then the poem's final prayer; "Grant us thy peace."

"Ebey's Lagoon" is the result of a return visit to Whidbey Island around Easter, 1984. Just north from the beach at Casey a gravel bar had created a stagnant pool of water which was suddenly breached by the sea, and the poem that results is something of an echo of "Christmas, Whidbey Island, 1975," which is also set at Casey. Loren considers the earlier poem the better, but I'm not so sure. This poem may not have the theological reach of the first, with its clear expression of Wilkinson's core ideas and beautiful use of language and form. But considered simply as poetry, this later work should not be discounted. I call as witness Robert Farrar Capon, in *An Offering of Uncles*:

I remember the first time I read Shakespeare's sonnets. "Lilies that fester smell far worse than weeds" stuck in my head for weeks—not so much for its meaning as for its marvellous *wordiness*...."

Not all men can draw, many men cannot sing, and the world is full of cooks who ought to be allowed to rise no higher than the scullery; but all men speak, and practically no one is immune to the delights of rhyme and reason. The child, as soon as he learns words, *plays* with words. The teen-ager, with his stock of current clichés and his mercurial pattern of jargon, is a poet. He may recite only commercial slogans and comparable idiocies; but he recites them, at least partly, because he loves the way the words rattle. And somewhere along the line he will, unless he is starved to death, come to love some very grand rattles indeed.

"Ebey's Lagoon" is noteworthy for its "marvelous wordiness," a tremendously specific study of a particular place and moment that glories in the taste and feel and sound of language. I'm aware that invoking Gerard Manley Hopkins might tend to diminish the poem at hand—what poem could stand up to that sort of comparison?—but I can't help hearing Loren's affinity for Hopkins in the dense, festering clusters of sound in the first three stanzas, and the release into something far lighter, fresher, freer in the last two. This is a very grand rattle indeed.

Again, read the poem aloud; what a fine warm-up this would be for an actor. Pay attention to patterns of sound, internal rhymes, the clatter of hard consonants, the lengths of words and lines and phrases. Four abrupt "b" words, followed immediately by all those tongue-pleasing "l" sounds, broken up by hard "k"s and "t"s:

> Below brown bluffs
> Ebey's lagoon
> Lay landlooped, rock-locked
> Silting tidelessly and long...

The whole first stanza is a single sustained sentence. The second is launched with a stripped-down six-syllable sentence of short, sharp words ("above silt flats / Flies bit") before it digs down into the stagnant lagoon itself, "When we dug that muck / The smell was rot and sulphur." But after three Holy Saturday paragraphs in those "brackish shallows," two witnesses come down, "To find the dead lagoon not brown / But fresh and flooding with the tide."

Suddenly, unexpectedly, the poem turns. It "Easters," to use a word that Hopkins made a verb, and the language lightens, rises like a resurrection. The flat horizontality of the brown lagoon gives way to the image of a tall, spindly heron, and everything lifts:

> Scoter skittered toward us
> In a spume of sunlit spray
> And a bright fish leaped from the bay's bright
> face...

As though, like Jesus in the Garden, "it had just come from some deep place." So maybe there's theology there after all.

It's difficult to pin down the exact the relationship between "Nightpaths" and the work of John Fowles, who is mentioned in the subtitle of the piece. Carl Jung's ideas about dreams and the shadow side of the psyche inspired Fowles' novel *The Magus*, and the poem's journey into the primal experiences of dreams—childhood, Adam, animality, wilderness—explores a similar landscape. There are other mythic literary influences informing the piece, similarly elusive in their precise point of connection, which is probably apt in a poem about the unconscious. In conversation about the piece, Loren commented that, "At night we become Everyman." We shed civilization and, like Max, head into the woods *Where the Wild Things Are*. He saw points of connection with the opening of George MacDonald's *Phantastes*, with *Finnegan's Wake*, and with C. S. Lewis's sense that human beings are not so far removed from other animals as we might flatter ourselves to think. There is also resonance with "Wreck Beach," where the dreamer sheds "book, clothes, mind, self," and wildness and wilderness are in tension with the reigned-in city: "Architecture, pavement, print, / All day I walk those lines with care..."

"Imago Mundi" is not a readily accessible poem, but Loren considers it his most important, central to his work and thought. Dense with ideas, it was composed in Cambridge toward the end of his sabbatical time there, an expression of the months of study and writing which are the beginnings of his book *Circles and the Cross*. Jürgen Moltmann's Gifford Lectures on natural theology had recently been published under the title of *God in Creation*, and the core ideas of that book inform the poem:

> Our starting point here is that all relationships which are analogous to God reflect the primal, reciprocal indwelling and mutual interpenetration of the trinitarian perichoresis: God *in* the world and the world *in* God; heaven and earth *in* the kingdom of God, pervaded by his glory; soul and body united *in* the life-giving Spirit to a human whole; woman and man *in* the kingdom of unconditional and unconditioned love, freed to be true and complete human beings... All living things—each in its own specific way—live in one another and with one another, from one another and for one another. 'Everything that lives / Lives not alone, nor for itself.' It is this trinitarian concept of life as interpenetration or perichoresis which will therefore determine this ecological doctrine of creation.

Clearly, Moltmann is exploring themes that have been foundational to Wilkinson's thought from the beginning, evident everywhere in Loren's poetry. God dwells in his creation *and* in human beings, who are part of that creation; not only all humanity but also the whole created world bear God's image and likeness, the *Imago Dei*. Wilkinson takes the idea further, exploring the ways in which we humans consequently bear the *imago mundi*, the image and likeness of the whole of creation, since God's image pervades it all. Our bodies and the body of the earth mirror each other, or, more precisely, bear a family resemblance. We are made of the same stuff; we are made of God.

Poets think in analogy and metaphor; they glory in seeing the reflection of one thing in another. What may seem to be a chance similarity of shape or colour may on closer examination reveal deeper or more complex resemblances, or even a profound inter-connectedness. It is no wonder that Moltmann's vision of the interpenetration of the three persons of the Trinity, and the interpenetration of God, humankind, and the created world, should resonate so powerfully with a poet. In the second stanza of "Imago Mundi," Wilkinson notices the similarity between earth and sky (the waters below and the waters above) in the star-like sparkle of "ice and air" in a Cambridge garden in a frosty early morning, and breathing them in, finds that his lung itself is a "dark-branched shrub." Then he zooms in to a microscopic level to show us how:

> ...iron rusts and rushes
> Blood-borne to my body's billion fires
> Whose fuel is the heavy ash of stars...

He is made of the stuff of stars; his body is itself a constellation, as is the garden he stands in. This realization:

> ...pushes
> Wordless blood to my unbound tongue

To praise: that the God of the cosmos
Let the heavens come to speech in me.

Just as God spoke Creation into being ("And God said, let there be..."), the Creation "comes to speech" in the poet's words of praise, stirred by this vision of the profound unity of all things.

The poem itself is an intricate interweaving of connected ideas, giving written expression to the complex patterns and relationships that make up God's creation. The conclusion of the second stanza ("the heavens come to speech in me") takes us right back to the first, and the creation-naming work of writers, scholars, gardeners:

Our task was still like Eve's and Adam's all day
long
To speak the light of language to the universe.

I love the homey little detail in that opening stanza where the birds themselves ask holy questions ("Light, Light, who let there be light?") and sing their own hymns of thanksgiving ("We are glad for the light and the worms in the grass"), a gift of holy speech heard only by the newly-wakened lovers, on the first morning of the week, on the first morning of Creation. I'm reminded of the first poem of this collection, where lion's song and hawk's speech are rendered dumb by Eve's transgression in the garden of Eden. It seems the New Adam and Eve can sometimes find themselves in a time before the Fall, in a New Creation where even the speech of animals is restored.

Just as there are endless patterns and structures underlying the universe—to the believer these are "the fingerprints of God," evidences of a Creator's design—so too the poet has shaped his poem around an intricate rhyme scheme that repeats in each stanza. Most rhyme is audible; we hear a rhyming couplet, or the ABAB pattern of a nursery rhyme, and it gives the kind of pleasure we experience in music: anticipation and resolution, and the delight of harmonious sounds. Internal rhymes make a poem sing, and a poem like "The Green Springs" uses very immediate juxtapositions of sound to create a sense of momentum. But no-one will hear the rhymes in "Imago Mundi." The reader will discover their pattern only through careful examination, just as the scientist finds the structures of creation through close and sustained attention. These discoveries provide another kind of satisfaction, the realization that there is a complex, satisfying pattern underlying the poem, that the poem's creator was working with a plan in mind. We recognize intentionality. And again, as we have seen with "Incarnicide" and "The Bloom of Carcinoma in His Bones," the use of complex formal patterns provides a means for the expression of feelings or ideas that would otherwise be difficult to craft into words.

Each eleven-line stanza of "Imago Mundi" begins and ends with a pair of unrhymed lines, further concealing the poem's shape from the casual reader. But the inner seven lines are carefully crafted; line 3 rhymes with line 9, line 4 with line 8, and so on. This pattern converges on itself until we reach the central line of each stanza, which has no rhyming partner; light, stars, ocean, plant, beasts, Man, and peace, essentially mapping the progress of the seven-day Creation story in Genesis.

This rhyme scheme is rare, perhaps because it contributes little to the tangible musicality (the "poetry") of a poem, being almost imperceptible. Loren cites Dylan Thomas as an inspiration, who used this structure in his 102-line "Author's Prologue" to the *Collected Poems 1934-1952*, culminating with a rhyming couplet at the exact centre. Structurally, such a poem essentially crosses itself. This is referred to as *chiastic* structure, from the Greek letter *chi*, which like our letter x is cross-shaped, and visually represents the way the rhymes converge toward the poem's centre, which is apt for an Easter poem.

But back to the poem at hand. The third stanza echoes the gathering of the seas to create dry land. The sea-wind that batters Cambridge on Wednesday "warms the land with sea-smell," reminding the poet that his blood is sea salt, his pink bones "basinning basalt," and that he is water and dust, woven "in the depths of earth and ocean." Its language and imagery are reminiscent of Loren's sea-shore poetry like "Ebey's Lagoon" or "Wedding on an Incoming Tide."

The fourth stanza connects the creation of plants and the garden of Eden with Maundy Thursday and the Garden of Gethsemane. Now "The gnarled gardener is older than the trunk he tends," and the imagery is of a choked pear-tree (a subtle reference to the cursed fig tree?), weed tendrils, acid seed, but with the hope "That dropped and rotting seeds may blossom yet from the dirt."

Stanzas five and six may be the finest in the piece. They are certainly the most tightly wrought, dense with references to the events of Good Friday and Holy Saturday, and carrying forward and expanding Loren's vision of gardens and gardeners. Stanza five immerses us in the events of Christ's crucifixion, interwoven with Old Testament sacrifice of birds and beasts, including the thicket-caught ram who stood in for Isaac. The poet finds the animals, gathered like fearful disciples at the edge of the action, "shaped like versions of myself in the forests of my sleep," which hearkens back to the opening of the poem (and foreshadows "Nightpaths," written a year later). The stanza's final two lines also refer back to those of stanza one:

> And no slain lamb or ram nor any blood of bull or
> dove
> Can give back the peace of our lost first task.

The body of Christ is laid in a tomb in another garden, and as Holy Saturday gives way to Easter Sunday, Wilkinson revisits the theme of his seminal poem "Gardener":

> He whom the Magdalene only could greet
> At first as the gardener. Exactly the image of
> God—
> Christ, who returned us the gardener's task.

The seventh stanza brings us to the seventh day of Creation and to the quiet of the garden early on Easter morning, when God the gardener rests and all creation waits in anticipation of new growth and the fulfillment of the great cosmic dance. Students in Loren's Regent summer courses at the Oregon Shakespeare Festival read E. M. W. Tillyard's book *The Elizabethan World Picture*, and saw the the celestial dance of stars and planets embodied in the stately, intricate Elizabethan dances on the Green before performances. Moltmann concludes *God in Creation* with "The World as Dance," quoting Gregory of Nyssa, "Once there was a time when the whole of rational creation formed a single dancing chorus looking upwards to the one leader of this dance," and Hippolytus' Easter hymn, "O thou leader of the mystic round-dance! O thou leader of the divine Pasch and new feast of all things!" before concluding: "The eternal perichoresis of the Trinity might also be described as an eternal round danced by the triune God, a dance out of which the rhythms of created beings who interpenetrate on another correspondingly rise like an echo."

"Imago Mundi" concludes with the image of garden and town "clean as a fleece," a suggestion that, ultimately, there will be a redemption and reconciliation of wilderness and city, of God's now-fallen Creation and man's flawed sub-creation, brought about by the Lamb of God. Significantly, the seventh stanza is the first one where the chiastic rhyme scheme is complete; even the opening and closing two lines are now part of the cross-shaped pattern (a dance?), converging on the word "peace."

"Hot Cross Buns," written at Easter, 1987, is a far more approachable poem that remembers Good Friday in Cambridge the year before. The three cross-shaped stanzas evoke Calvary, but they don't dwell on Crucifixion. Mostly this is a comforting poem, framed with the memory of an early morning trip to an English bakery to buy a dozen buns, "cut with a cross & round as time," reminiscent of the Celtic cross, and the book he began at Cambridge, *Circles and the Cross*. He sees the Cross at the centre of the circle of creation, and the union of circle and cross suggests multiple layers of meaning to Loren. It is an expression of the unity of earth and heaven, time and eternity, science and faith, the cycle of the seasons and the church year.

In Loren and Mary Ruth Wilkinson's book *Caring for Creation in Your Own Backyard* (1992), they ask, "Can the two symbols—of the earth (a circle) and the cross—be reconciled?"

> We are convinced the answer to these questions is yes.... But first we need to think a little more about what is implied by these two symbols, circle and cross, and the relationships and tensions between them.
>
> First the circle. The earth is round, and it is full of cycles. Living things die and rot into soil, which nourishes more living things. Rain falls on mountains, where it drains into rivers, which flow into the sea, which evaporates into clouds, which carry rain again to the mountains.... For all these cycles the circle is a good symbol.
>
> Christian thinking is centred on the cross. Geometrically, the cross is the intersection of two straight lines, a horizontal and a vertical. Instead of one line, turning again and again in a circle, the Christian sees that the earth is not eternal. For another line inter-

sects ours from outside. The cross refers to the place where God's perspective has intersected ours most clearly. The execution of one man at a particular place and time is the midpoint, the crux: the intersection of eternal and temporal, God's time and ours.

The biblical view [expressed in the book of Ecclesiastes] recognizes the reality of the cycles of nature. . . . And though within those cycles of the earth there is room for every kind of activity, God has 'set eternity in the hearts of men.' We are not satisfied with the cycles. For all the beauty of the earth and its circling life, it does not bring its own meaning with it.

It is only when we think of the earth as 'creation' that we can think rightly about caring for it. The circle, in its completeness, is a good symbol for creation. But it is also a zero, a cipher, an emptiness. So perhaps we can learn from an ancient Christian symbol, the circle centered on the cross. Sometimes it is known as the Celtic Cross. It expresses a profound truth: the God whom we meet in Christ at the cross is also the God of creation. And just as the arms of the cross enclose and intersect the circle, so also Redemption includes creation.

In "Hot Cross Buns," the homely image of a hot cross bun provides a glimpse of the peaceable kingdom where the circle and the cross combine, where creation and redemption meet in the fullness of time:

This hot bread
Holds the crux,
This centre in
The cycles where
All ways start.

"The Seal" is remarkable not for its intricacies or its ideas, but for the potent effect of its direct, deeply felt re-counting of a quiet death. The painfully specific details of the seal's dying are reminiscent of the passage in "Incarni-cide" cited above:

So we watched it ebb in joy and pain
Waded out and fetched the seal,
Laid it on the pebbled beach:
Stroked the warm, smooth skin,
Shuddering with its breath:
And lest the beautiful, cruel gulls
Should tear it as it drifted, dying
Hit it twice behind the head
With a staff of rotting alder wood.

The two acts of killing are very different: one a horrif-ic crime, the other a severe act of mercy. But both poems evoke in the reader a complex mix of feelings. "Incarni-cide" acknowledges, however uncomfortably, that even in a murderer who kills his wife, there can also be a confused and conflicted sort of love. In "The Seal" we flinch at the act of killing, even though this death is an expression of kindness, provoked by a recognition of the cruelty in nature.

That same cove by the Wilkinsons' house at Hunterston farm is the setting for "Wedding on an Incoming Tide," another poem that tells the story of an event with tremendous clarity and effect. As family and friends set up for daughter Heidi's wedding:

> The tide went out and out
> Till algae shone green as a lawn on the rocks
> And starfish clumped and drooped in the sun
> As though the sea were gone for good.

Hardly a setting for the beautiful seaside ceremony they had imagined. And as preparations continue, the poet cannot help monitoring the continued ebbing of the sea. The poem returns again and again to the discouraging reports on the fall of the tide, steady as the waves, stanza after stanza: "We set up tables for a feast / And watched the sea recede."

As the tide continues to go out, the poet finds poetry in a commonplace expression:

> The mud flats stank to heaven
> And stranded clams beneath the sand
> Expelled their prayers....

He comes to see the exposed mud flats as a bleak metaphor for hard realities of human experience that belie the hopeful wishes of a wedding day:

But we readied for a wedding
Though still the tide went out;
Across a century of broken things
Begun in hope: marriages and homes and children
Stranded like fish on the drying stones
When the sea of faith withdrew.

But when faith and the tide reach their lowest ebb, the wedding guests arrive, and hope begins to return, signalled by the poem's first rhyme;

As the tide of friends walked down the hill
The cove began to fill.

The tidal reports continue, but now turned to celebration and reassurance. In due time the swells break higher on the rocks, and the poem shifts subtly but dramatically from past tense to present, flowering from a tone of anxious observation to the faith of a father's matrimonial blessing, which ultimately returns to Wilkinson's grand theme:

And as you stand before us on the deck
And pledge your faithfulness till death
The cool sea has returned.

Hear this, then, both of you;
However far the sea recedes, keep faith:
And he who daily fills this cove with life
Will never leave you gasping on the sand;

His blood is the life of the circling sea.
His life is yours.

This poem is very much a partner to "Wedding in October," nearly a decade earlier. They are brave and honest poems, where the promise of marriage is held juxtaposed with the realistic but rarely spoken knowledge that not all weddings work, not all marriages thrive or survive. Both poems draw metaphors from nature to show abundance and lack, life and death, joy and struggle in tension: a river full of spawning, dying salmon, and the emptying of a sea cove that strands its creatures and reveals "broken and abandoned things." But both ultimately affirm that, in the words of the earlier poem, "not all vows break." The two poems find their resolution in the same place, the sacrificial body and blood of Christ:

> For they are built together in one whose own vows
> never broke;
> Christ, who broke his body for this dying world's
> life,
> As they give soul and body as a husband, as a wife.

The remaining poems in the collection continue to be about family and friends, and are often celebrations of birth. The first three also mark the turning of the Liturgical year: Epiphany, Lent, All Saints Day.

Coming right after Christmas and the celebration of Jesus' birth, Epiphany is the feast of Light, of God revealed in Christ. "The Sundays after Epiphany" is an evocative portrait of early mornings in the winter on Galiano, and the slow coming of light, culminating on the drive home from church when:

> In the dark of our daughter's womb
> The child kicks against the dark,
> The touch as warm and sudden as the sun.

"Womb-Words" is a Lenten poem, written for the artist Dunstan Massey, who lives and works as part of the Benedictine community at Westminster Abbey in Mission, British Columbia. Lent is a time of anticipation, of preparation for Easter, and this is a poem about the slow process of bringing things to fruition: a sculpture, a newly planted field, or a baby. I love the parallel between the young monks who "are throwing manure / Into a spreader for the pasture" and the old monk who "Throws plaster over / Fresh clay forms of angels." Garden-making and art-making are both hard work, body work, and so is the work of forming a child in a womb. Father Massey crafts a sculpture of angels, "Arched in a silent dance to welcome / A woman and the Word within her womb," and the poem culminates in a celebration of all this nurturing, all this labour, all this fertility:

> ...round the Word was the silence
> Fertile as a waiting womb
> Of the plaster angel-mold;
> Rich as the newly-manured roots of this hill:
> Wordless on an afternoon in Lent.

Notes

All Saints Day is the day after Hallowe'en (All Hallows' Eve), at the end of the Church Year and after harvest is done. "Sowing on All Saints Day" has Loren the gardener plowing under the remains of the summer crop, "All that green and summer fountaining / back into the stony soil," and planting for the first time a cover crop of winter rye. It is an act of faith, a foreshadowing of a resurrection that will, if all goes well, begin to show itself in the spring. He enters the warm house:

> in hope,
> only in hope:
>
> that my ten thousand buried seeds will sprout,
> that in some unimaginable summer
>
> the field will be a multitude of new grain,
> ripe, rejoicing in the wind.

The final two poems also commemorate births, but look backward rather than forward. Two specific births, those of his son Erik and his daughter Heidi.

"Forty Years" commemorates Erik's fortieth birthday. A great delight in Wilkinson's poetry is his experimentation with structure, often in poems that involve great feeling. Here, each stanza is made up of forty syllables, each arranged in five lines of increasing length. This lends the piece a subtle rhythmic pulse, a repeated pattern of slow expansion and regathering, like breathing in and exhaling. Interestingly, the final stanza inverts that shape, opening with a twelve syllable line and closing with four simple one-syllable words. I asked Loren if this was to give the poem a sense of closure, of bringing things to a point. He replied, "It just seemed the thing to do."

It is moving to see a father attend so closely to the narrative of his son's life, for the reader to enter into that kind of empathy. How fascinating to see a man of words—a literary scholar, a writer, a poet—imagine the early childhood of his son, who was born with almost no hearing.

> You did not hear
> Those first three years of life
> So grew up in a wordless world
> Of touch and watching (body, lips and eyes)
> Till batteries and wire linked you to the rest of us.

Notice the movement in Loren's consideration of words and silence over the course of forty years worth of poems. The first piece in this volume imagines an Eden where even the animals have the gift of language, until it is taken from them in the Fall. Twenty years later he imagines it restored to them in another garden, in Cambridge (though "it was only we who heard their chirp as words: their praise was wordless as their wonderment"). Before tending the garden of Eden, Adam's great task is naming creation, and Loren marvels that "the God of the cosmos / Let the heavens come to speech in me." Words are the snowshoe webbing whose "careful shapes will hold you up." But they are not always spoken words: the old ones carved God's words in Raven shapes in cedar before the coming of Christianity, and "God spoke here in Raven's croak." At Epiphany, considering the child growing in his daughter's womb, he contemplates the Word that became flesh and dwelt among us. This time it is a silent word, the same Word that Father Dunstan's stone angels celebrate in a silent dance, while "The monks work wordlessly, with care." Apart from this poem for Erik, Loren's last word on the subject is in a quiet orchard outside the monastery, as though even the hazelnuts and pears have taken a vow of silence:

> In the beginning was the Word:
> But round the Word was the silence
> Fertile as a waiting womb
> Of the plaster angel-mold;
>
> Rich as the newly-manured roots of this hill:
> Wordless on an afternoon in Lent.

But God spoke creation into being, and John's gospel refers to Christ as the Word. So for Erik:

> Words lived in books
> But not between people.
> Even God was theoretical,
> But things were real: the sea, the trees, the rock...

He moves away to Hong Kong and discovers that his "gift of wordless listening and speech / Could lead this urban age's children nearer home." In time Erik himself returns home, and the great truth at the heart of the poem is that for Erik, a man of doing rather than speaking, "God is less a theory" than a Reality that does not necessarily require words.

The first half of the poem spans decades; it is the survey of forty years of life. But at this point the poem steps into Erik's world, becomes utterly concrete and experiential. Father and son climb together to a stone peak above "the glacier's great white throne," and Erik unfurls a kite, "Writing on air" and "Reading the wind (*spiritus, ruach elohim*)." The Spirit, the breath of God. The stanza that follows is an extraordinary exclamation of transcendence, epiphany: it offers up a moment of wordless joy, of pure experience, in some of the most glorious words the poet has written:

The gift of things,
Pouring down, pouring down,
Like torrents on the sculpted rock,
Like trickles from the snow beneath our feet
Like deep green blueberry leaves flared by frost to
    flame.

Another perfect moment, a small epiphany, is captured in the last poem in the book, "A Provence Annunciation," which also uses shaped stanzas. It was written as a birthday gift for Loren's daughter Heidi, and recalls time together in the south of France. "It was a perfect visit. You dream this kind of thing." With Heidi's two daughters they visited an abandoned fourteenth century chapel in an olive orchard a short bike ride from where they were staying. The outside of the little stone church is adorned with sculptures of notable appearances of the angel Gabriel: the sword driving Adam and Eve from the garden, angels shutting the mouths of the lions in the lions' den, and a whole panel about the Annunciation, when the angel came to Mary and told her that she would have a son who would be the Messiah. The chapel was locked. Above the immense red door was a round open window, with carvings of the angel and the Lamb of God. Through a slit in the door, Mary Ruth photographed a glorious shaft of light that caught the dust particles inside the ancient church and made them shimmer.

As the adults stood looking at the carvings, from inside the empty chapel emerged the sound of girls' voices, singing "Breathe On Me, Breath Of God" in perfect harmony. Heidi's two daughters, accomplished singers, had found a slit in the wall and began singing through it, projecting their voices into the sanctuary:

Outside, in the sun, we hear the choir:
Their silver voices fill the space like the light

That poured
It's molten sword
Through the high round window
Beneath the limestone lamb of God.
And still, on the road to Arles the traffic roared.

Notes

The simple beauty and musicality of this final image stands as a fitting postlude to the rich celebration of language, imagery, theology, and humanity that has gone before. The stillness of the ancient garden chapel fills with glorious song, but always against the counterpoint of technology and the distant city.

Ron Reed
Vancouver, BC

CPSIA information can be obtained
at www.ICGtesting.com
Printed in the USA
FSOW01n0515120717
36056FS